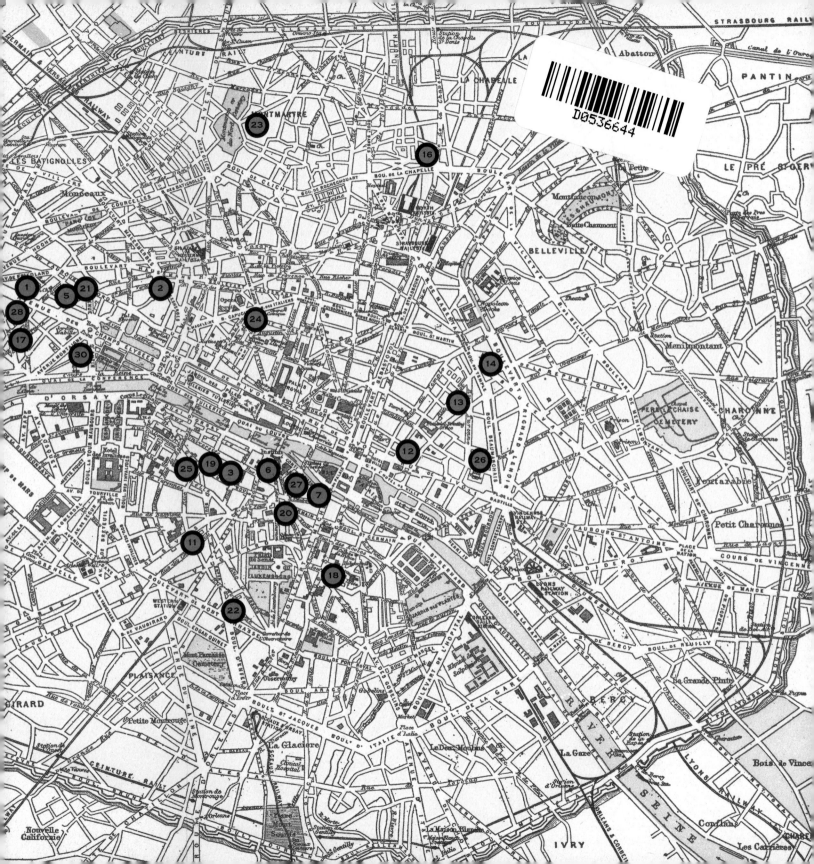
D0536644

PARISIAN HIDEAWAYS

PARISIAN HIDEAWAYS

*Exquisite Rooms
in Enchanting Hotels*

CASEY O'BRIEN BLONDES

photography by **BÉATRICE AMAGAT**

RIZZOLI
NEW YORK

First published in the United States of America in 2009
by Rizzoli International Publications, Inc.
300 Park Avenue South
New York, NY 10010
www.rizzoliusa.com

© 2008 Casey O'Brien Blondes

Photography © 2008 Béatrice Amagat

All rights reserved. No part of this publication may be reproduced, stored in a
retrieval system, or transmitted in any form or by any means, electronic, mechanical,
photocopying, recording, or otherwise, without prior consent of the publishers.

2009   2010   2011   2012 / 10   9   8   7   6   5   4   3   2   1

Distributed in the U.S. trade by Random House, New York

Printed in China

ISBN-13: 978-0-8478-3214-9

Library of Congress Catalog Control Number: 2008939324

PREVIOUS SPREAD:
**Opulent Jacques Garcia-
designed dining room,
L'Hôtel**

FOR JEFFREY

*WHO INTRODUCED ME TO PARIS
AND CHOSE THAT FIRST HOTEL.*

SINCERE THANKS
to my invaluable agent Charlotte Sheedy
and her talented team Meredith Kaffel and Hillary Costa.
Merci to Béatrice Amagat for her artistic vision and
camaraderie and Kathleen Jayes for her expert touch.

CONTENTS

OPPOSITE:
Hotel du Petit Moulin
occupies an historic
Marais bakery.

INTRODUCTION

$\mathscr{E}$VERYONE HAS HIS OR HER FANTASY of an ideal hotel, and Paris, being *Paris* (with everything it symbolizes in the collective imagination), is the object of particularly exalted expectation. We should know better, but many of us—not just romantics and optimists—persist in hoping that reality will meet desire. Fortunately Paris is spoiled for choice when it comes to exceptional hotels. The question is how to choose.

In his book *Paris*, John Russell, former chief art critic for the *New York Times*, cautions: "Hotels, like restaurants, are a subject upon which advice is usually fatal. The choice of an hotel is as private a matter as the choice of a wife." With this in mind, I gave up on impartiality and set out to find thirty hotels where I'd like to stay.

Because Paris is among the world's most beautiful cities, aesthetics were a major determinant but whether a décor is minimalist, eclectic, or historic it had to be inherently Parisian. Being quintessentially Parisian is as much about spirit as style and above all describes an environment where you wake up knowing you could only be in Paris—not Sydney, Toronto, or Dubrovnik.

A distinctive hotel reflects the taste and personality of its owner. For this reason, all but two of the selections are family- or sole-proprietor–owned and most are owner managed. Not by chance French creators designed them. An impressive roster of interior architects, artists, and couturiers collaborated with owners on design concepts, yet no hotel feels like a designer showcase. Needs of

OPPOSITE:
View across Paris from top floor guest room, Pont Royal.

1

guests take precedence over creative bravura, and when an element disappoints it is reworked in the interest of creating an environment where clients feel at ease.

My vision of an idyllic Parisian location is a calm side street rather than a broad avenue or busy intersection. Parisian hideaways are discreet destinations often with minimal or no signage—where one's privacy is protected. Only the Raphael, a favorite with diplomats, made the cut despite flags flying above the entrance. *Hideaway* also suggests a degree of intimacy and personal contact, which eliminates *palace* hotels (all of which are currently owned by international chains) and franchises.

Many of the selections refer to themselves as "boutique hotels," since the term *small* connotes diminutive room size. The trend in boutique hotels is quite the opposite, and many have undergone recent renovation to reduce capacity in favor of enlarging guest rooms. Maximum capacity is well under a hundred rooms and averages between fifteen and forty.

Wary of labels such as *hôtel de charme*, and "home away from home," which have lost credibility from overuse, and niches like hip, romantic, or design that can overlook the importance of comfort and service, I tried to include a cross section of ambiances representative of the many facets of Paris and its inhabitants. Hotels are grouped by theme rather than arrondissement, permitting a search for a destination by décor, special interest, or passing fancy.

I expected to discover broader geographic distribution, but prime hotel real estate remains central, with Saint-Germain in the 6th on the Left Bank of the Seine and the "golden triangle" in the 8th between the Champs-Élysées, Avenue Georges V, and Avenue Montaigne on the Right Bank having the highest concentration of hotels that met my criteria. The Marais is also well represented, and there are a number of selections in the teens, particularly the sixteenth. Many close contenders were omitted in the interest of diversity. After visiting close to two hundred hotels I feel satisfied that despite the subjectivity of personal bias, it is a fair selection.

The most gratifying dividend of extensive shoe-leather reporting was getting to know the people who operate these wonderful hotels. They are a dedicated and good-natured group. Contrary to the popular myth of French arrogance, staff is consistently warm and welcoming. Exceptions were inevitable, but I concluded that hotel personnel enjoy a high level of job satisfaction. Not only do they like what they do, but much of their pleasure is derived from yours.

Another bit of encouraging news is that despite a strong euro, Paris hotel rates remain good value compared those of many capital cities. Because of fluctuating exchange rates and seasonal modifications, room rates are listed on a comparative basis as either *moderate, mid-price,* or *luxury.* Only the Raphael, with suite accommodations for a head of state, is classified *deluxe.* Services are improving all the time. Air conditioning, wi-fi, mp3 speaker stands, and flat-screen televisions are becoming standard features, and even hotels with fewer than fifty rooms are likely to have a fitness room and sauna. Most small hotels do not have a restaurant, but those that do tend to have a great chef. The Pont Royal, l'Hôtel, and Relais Saint-Germain are worth staying at just to guarantee a dinner reservation. Lounge bars are another welcome trend, as is twenty-four-hour room service.

The most valuable resource a Parisian hideaway has to offer is the knowledge and rich culture of its owner and management. They know their neighborhood and relish sharing its secrets with guests. Because staff turnover is low, you will find that everyone is a possible source for tips and recommendations. There is a good chance your stay will engender an ongoing friendship, as these hotels, like the city they encapsulate, foster fidelity. It's hard to find someone who has visited Paris and doesn't dream of returning.

NOTE ON PRICING

Room rate categories are based on the range for a double (standard to superior), though the charge is usually lower for a single person. Many hotels straddle categories.

MODERATE: between 100 and 190 euros
MID-PRICE: between 190 and 370 euros
LUXURY: between 370 and 600 euros
DELUXE: 450 euros and above.

This is a rough guideline and it is best to consult hotel web sites for a complete list of rates and services. Most hotels have seasonal rate adjustments and many offer promotional packages and online booking discounts. Rates and complete contact info are included in the Hotel Index, pages 210–213.

OPPOSITE CLOCKWISE FROM TOP LEFT:
Shimmering metallic leaf paneling, Châteaubriand dining room.

Antique bird-cage, Saint Vincent.

Tea for two, sitting room of Windsor Home.

Breakfast room, Le Lavoisier.

Brocante chic

CHÂTEAUBRIAND
(8th), Champs-Élysées
Eighteenth-century elegance

LE LAVOISIER
(8th), Saint-Augustin
Tailored with a twist

SAINT VINCENT
(7th), Musée d'Orsay
Updated bourgeois

WINDSOR HOME
(16th), Passy
High-style retro

Those of us hooked on browsing flea markets and antiques shops will recognize kindred spirits in the proprietors of the Brocante Chic selections. In France, collectors enamored of the patina of previously owned treasures are called *chineurs*, and what better way to display one's best finds than in a hotel, where a wide audience can appreciate them?

Each owner has a favored style, type of collectible, or epoch, but all are willing to tolerate the incursion of an exceptional anomaly. The Châteaubriand has the highest concentration of valuable historic loot—windows, banisters, parquet, wrought iron, and wood paneling sourced from historic properties and acquired through a network of dealers and auctioneers.

The Saint Vincent in Saint-Germain showcases the bourgeois charm of "revisited" Napoléon III. The Lavoisier's owners opted for tightly edited placement of late-nineteenth- and early-twentieth-century decorative objects and paintings within a neoclassic interior to inject character and a whiff of nostalgia. Windsor Home exudes funky eclecticism created through witty juxtaposition of furniture and artwork with punchy paint and fabric schemes. If you are inspired to hunt for take-home treasure, be sure to schedule time for a visit to the *puces*, flea markets on the outskirts of the city.

CHÂTEAUBRIAND

*Eighteenth-century elegance
off the Champs-Élysées*

Romain Rio
6, rue Châteaubriand
75008 Paris
www.hotelchateaubriand.com

OPPOSITE:
Intimate chinoiserie-
themed salon with
hand embroidered
silk wallcovering.

RUE CHÂTEAUBRIAND is somewhat of an anomaly for a street wedged between the Étoile and Champs-Élysées: few cars, fewer pedestrians, and not a shop in sight. A cluster of hotels share the privilege of being just beyond range of the nonstop action this part of the 8th arrondissement is known for, and the stately Chamber of Commerce mansion sits discreetly within a walled garden taking up much of the block.

Romain Rio, a connoisseur of exclusivity in its many guises, knew the Châteaubriand had the makings of greatness when he snatched it up in 2005. He has a second hotel around the corner, but the Châteaubriand has become his Pygmalion and if anyone can convince him that renovation has a beginning and an end, he might agree that his five-story Eliza is ready for her presentation at court.

Rio is reluctant to share with guests the provenance of scores of treasures he entrusted five antiques dealers to hunt down in auction houses and attics. He prefers that the quality of the environment exert a subconscious influence—prompting guests to think, "I feel great at the Châteaubriand." Rio insists that every aesthetic choice is based on how it enhances the pleasure of his guests, but it's unlikely they share quite the same standards.

A mirror from the Château de Chambord, a bull's-eye window from Versailles, stairway carpeting from the French presidential palace, towel racks from the Orient Express . . . the list goes on. Rio has a weakness for eighteenth-century style, announced by the period *boiseries* and wrought-iron grille (now fully automated) of the entryway.

A jewel-box salon sits to the right of the entry hall illuminated by an enormous chandelier. Behind exquisite carved doors, the walls of the chinoiserie-themed retreat are covered in hand-embroidered silk. Despite its Oriental appearance, a Frenchwoman did the custom embroidery in Paris. Three miniature hand-painted butterflies flutter out from under the rug across eighteenth-century parquet. One-of-a-kind painted vignettes appear in unexpected corners throughout the hotel and are among the many ways Rio customizes rooms.

A broad stone staircase sweeps down from the reception room to a garden patio, salon, and dining room. A two-story wrought-iron-and-glass wall extending

ABOVE, LEFT TO RIGHT:

Detail, painted
ornamental mirror,
chinoiserie salon.

Detail, dining room.

Dramatic floral
arrangement reflected
in eighteenth-century
mirror, entry hall.

OPPOSITE TOP:

Guestrooms feature artful
arrangements of period
paintings or prints above
headboards.

OPPOSITE BOTTOM RIGHT:

Reception lounge
with view onto interior
garden patio.

OPPOSITE BOTTOM LEFT:

A novel, marble-lined
bathing area is
incorporated within
room 10.

up through the reception area encloses the patio. An indoor-outdoor effect is created through a curved, glass-paneled wall that slides open by retracting into the wall of the dining room. An oversize mirror in an ornate frame hangs on the rear wall of the patio, providing added depth. Having managed a restaurant in the 17th, Rio is expanding the hotel's services to include an intimate bistro. Naturally, the Royal Limoges porcelain used for breakfast is a custom Louis XVI–inspired design.

No two guest rooms are alike, and the décor of each landing corridor also varies. Eighteenth- and nineteenth-century prints hung in sets are a recurrent motif. In guest rooms they tend to be arranged in groupings above the headboard, often with a carved and gilded wood pediment crowning the effect. Powdery colors and soft neutrals predominate in bedrooms. There are no suites, but most rooms have generous seating areas with beautifully upholstered armchairs and couches. The black lacquer wardrobe fronted with glass panes resembles a display cabinet. Bedside tables, lamps, and wall sconces are artfully coordinated.

Rio's fondness for Bourbon grandeur is balanced with an appreciation for technological refinement. An entertainment exclusive with MGM studios supplies the hotel with three film releases per month—just two months following general release (airlines wait four to five for theirs). Laundry is done on the premises to ensure it is handled correctly, as well as delicately scented.

The Rio family is from Brittany, and Rio's parents owned hotels in Angers, La Baule, and Paris. Madame Rio senior, known for impeccable taste, remains an active sounding board for her thirty-three-year-old son. Ghislaine, the attentive manager, worked at the hotel under previous ownership and was hired back by Rio after they worked together at another establishment. "Meticulous" is how Ghislaine describes her boss (with a smile), "but very kind and always ready to *rendre service*." One couldn't ask for more.

ROMAN RIO'S COUPS DE COEUR

RESTAURANT
PIERRE GAGNAIRE

6, rue Balzac, 75008

Tel.: 01 58 36 12 50 | p.gagnaire@wanadoo.fr

Gagnaire is the most iconoclastic of the city's three-star chefs, and Rio admires his ability to incorporate strains of international cuisine while remaining resolutely French. Regional fusion cooking at its most refined.

BOUTIQUE—MENSWEAR AND ACCESSORIES
LOUIS VUITTON

101, avenue des Champs-Élysées, 75008

Tel.: 08 10 81 00 10

Monday–Saturday, 10:00 A.M.–8:00 P.M.; Sunday, 11:00 A.M.–7:00 P.M.

Marc Jacobs seems to have hit his stride with his menswear collection, which is trendy without being gimmicky. Everything an urban dandy needs, from scooter helmet to briefcase.

BOUTIQUE—WATCHES
DUBAIL

66, rue François 1er, 75008

Tel.: 01 53 57 47 00 | www.dubail.fr

Monday–Saturday, 10:00 A.M.–6:30 P.M.

The ultimate selection including unusual custom Rolex models.

BOUTIQUE—WOMENSWEAR, MENSWEAR AND ACCESSORIES
HERMÈS

42, avenue Georges V, 75008

Tel.: 01 47 20 48 51

When Hermès purchased the hat maker Motsch, the company converted Motsch's beautiful Old World shop into an Hermès boutique. The standard for craftsmanship, design, and timeless French elegance.

BOUTIQUE—DESIGNER WOMENSWEAR
GUY LAROCHE

35, rue François 1er, 75008

Tel.: 01 53 23 01 82

For flattering and colorful cocktail dresses, which Guy Laroche does to perfection.

LE LAVOISIER

Tailored with a twist

Michel Bouvier
21, rue Lavoisier
75008 Paris
www.hotellavoisierparis.com

OPPOSITE:
Black-lacquer end tables, sunflower-yellow walls, and coral-pink carpeting evoke an art deco, surrealist palette.

*I*F YOU TELL FRIENDS AT HOME you're staying around Saint-Augustin (which is what a Parisian would say) you are unlikely to see nods of recognition, but so much the better—this unexpected neighborhood can be your discovery, along with a hotel to match. Hardly lost yet located just far enough beyond the 8th arrondissement business hub to escape the bustle, rue Lavoisier gives onto avenues quickly leading to the Opéra, Madeleine, and the Champs-Élysées.

Owner Michel Bouvier is a minor legend among Parisian hoteliers, having arrived from Savoie as a penniless teen and worked his way from waiter to successful restaurateur on fashionable rue due Cherche Midi in the 6th. He opened his first confidential hotel, le St-Grégoire, to satisfy clients wanting a place to stay where they felt as good as they did eating at his restaurant. Eighteen years later, he created his fourth hotel, in an area overlooked by boutique hotels.

Evidently, his clientele was waiting, as the Lavoisier has been a solid hit since opening in 1999, and today 65 percent of guests are repeat clients, many of whom return several times a year. They come for the hotel's appealing formula of restrained elegance, excellent personnel, and accessible location. Designer Jean-Philippe Nuel has used clean lines and inventive color choices to create a fresh neoclassic interior, respectful of the building's nineteenth-century character. Though the elevator has been relocated from the central stairwell, its decorative cage was preserved, along with the lofty room proportions of the period.

Nuel contrasts traditional painted wainscoting and wood shutters with vivid sunflower-yellow walls and deep coral carpeting. Guest room furniture sheathed in tailored cotton and linen slipcovers and beds with pristine white blanket covers impart a sense of cleanliness and rigor. Flower-print curtains and deco-influenced Nuel-designed furniture strike subtle retro notes. Michel Bouvier and partner Madame Agaud inject warmth and individuality through skillful placement of chests of drawers, mirrors, lamps, and artwork they collect at flea markets. Each object is carefully considered for the decorative counterpoint it provides in an otherwise pared-down décor—a hallmark of twentieth-century French interior design after the charged ornamentation of the Belle Époque.

There are several front rooms with balconies and one on the back side of the building that has an ultra private terrace. Rooms on the street side get plenty of natural daylight.

The ground floor has three sitting-area options, the coziest of which is the secluded library bar furnished with a comfy leather sofa and shelves lined with antique hand-bound literary classics. The *sous sol* breakfast rooms have warm ochre walls. The main room features a much-photographed vintage poster entitled *La Vigne*, featuring a bacchanalian vision of postwar grape harvesting.

Experienced staff do their best to ensure a stress-free visit. Manager Ludovic Peressini has created a hotel blog where guests can fill in simple questionnaires so that personnel can arrange train tickets and transportation to and from the airport along with numerous other services. The staff is up-to-date on the best services, shops, and neighborhood restaurants as well as current cultural events, and the Lavoisier is ideally placed for shopping, as well as for attending concerts, museum shows, and ballet performances at Opéra Garnier.

For Parisian style encapsulating the essence of less-is-more chic, in a neighborhood that taps into the authentic working tempo of the city, the Lavoisier is your destination of choice.

GOURMET PRODUCE
HÉDIARD

21, place de la Madeleine, 75008

Tel.: 01 43 12 88 88 | www.hediard.fr

Purveyor since 1854 of domestic and imported delicacies, with a better fresh produce selection than Fauchon across the square. Gorgeous presentation and well-informed staff.

BOUTIQUE—TOYS
LE BONHOMME DE BOIS

43, boulevard Malesherbes, 75008

Tel.: 01 40 17 03 33 | www.bonnehommedebois.com

Directly opposite the hotel is a toy store, specializing in wood and fabric toys, that also stocks furniture, costumes, and crafts.

RESTAURANT, TEA SALON, AND GALLERY
1728

8, rue d'Anjou, 75008

Tel.: 01 40 17 07 77 | www.restaurant-1728.com

Jean-François Chuet and his wife, classical musician Yang Lining, lovingly restored a suite of eighteenth-century drawing rooms in the former 1728 mansion of General Marquis Lafayette into an original salon environment that incorporates works of art, a restaurant, and a tea salon. Cuisine with Asian accents and a wine list featuring natural sulphite-free vintages. Lining is a tea specialist, and Chuet is resident *antiquaire*.

RESTAURANT
SENDERENS

9, place de la Madeleine, 75008

Tel.: 01 42 65 22 90 | www.sederens.fr | restaurant@senderens.fr

After twenty years as the chef-proprietor of Lucas Carton, Alain Sederens decided it was time to put his name over the door and open up to a larger clientele. He modernized the interior, added a tapas and sushi bar, and shook up the traditional gastronomic menu. The exquisite wood paneling and culinary excellence are still in place, but the prim white tablecloths are gone, replaced by sensual contemporary furnishings and a correspondingly lighter *addition*.

TEA SALON
LA CHARLOTTE DE L'ISLE

24, rue St.-Louis-en-l'Isle, 75004

Tel.: 01 45 54 25 83 | www.la-charlotte.fr

A whimsical café serving divine hot chocolate and sundry chocolate confections, presided over since 1972 by Sylvie Langlet and her ceramic puppets. Wednesday performances with a snack menu for children.

SAINT VINCENT

Updated bourgeois

Bertrand Plasmans
5, rue du Pré-aux-Clercs
75007 Paris
www.hotel-st-vincent.com

OPPOSITE:
A fire in the salon's open hearth creates a cozy ambiance in the late afternoon and evening.

*S*OME HOTELS HAVE ALL THE LUCK—looks, location, and legacy. Which explains the smile on owner-director Bertrand Plasman's face as he recounts the restoration of his treasure, a gracious bourgeois residence in the Left Bank, Cour Carrée antiques district between boulevard Saint-Germain and the Seine. Plasman happened to be the owner of a charming two-star hotel, Saint Thomas d'Aquin, next door, so when he acquired number 5, rue du Pré-aux-Clercs, he knew he had a winner.

The warm beige stone facade of the early-nineteenth-century mansion is carved with classical cornices above the widows, pilasters framing massive coach-way doors, and lovely garlands of flowers. The lobby and ground-floor salon occupy a former central courtyard, where horse-drawn carriages once dispatched aristocratic passengers in total discretion. The covered passageway was preserved, so guests enter the hotel through a series of doorways landscaped with slender hornbeam trees, clipped boxwoods, and flowering branches in antique urns—a gentrified mise-en-scène that sets the tone for the refined interior. Saint Vincent is a cultured haven spiced with romance and nostalgia, a quintessentially Parisian environment that appeals to a broad range of tastes.

The salon makes one feel you are in an elegant private residence. Two generous couches and a pair of armchairs face a stone chimney with over-mantel that is lit every afternoon, late fall through early spring. The decorative objects, mirrors, and artwork tend to be antique, while much of the updated traditional furniture upholstered in warm grays and browns accented with berry were sourced at Mise en Demure on rue du Cherche-Midi in the 6th arrondissement. The parquet-and-flagstone floor is covered with area rugs and it is evident that close attention was paid to marrying old and new elements using a subtle range of pattern, texture, and patina. Plasman describes the look he has created as "Napoleon III revisited."

The concern for comfort expressed in the French decorative arts of the second half of the nineteenth century has definitely been honored at the Saint Vincent. Bathrooms are richly appointed in marble, and fabric for guest-room curtains and bedcovers were selected from the finest French textile collections located right in the neighborhood along rues Bonaparte and de Furstenberg.

Room 471 under the eaves has a great tub and tons of natural light. Rooms on the first floor have tall windows with wood shutters, and rooms on the third and top floors overlooking the road have balconies. While ceilings are lower on the top floor, the balconies are wider and offer an ideal vantage point for an intimate alfresco breakfast.

Rooms to the rear of the building overlook a bright inner courtyard landscaped with a pair of birch trees and tidy boxwoods. Abundant yet informal floral arrangements inject refreshing country charm throughout the ground floor and typify the lack of pretension and sure taste that characterizes the Saint Vincent. The breakfast room has a selection of excellent informal portraits by Luc Fournol taken in the early 1960s of Jeanne Moreau, Alain Delon, and a boyish Yves Saint Laurent sketching "New Look" models when he started with Dior. Wooden benches, hand-carved three-legged chairs, and bistro tables set with red-and-white striped Basque linens create a relaxed, countrified ambiance echoed in a healthful breakfast including organic yogurt and fresh fruit salad.

Afternoon tea is served before the fire, followed by the appearance of a well-stocked drinks trolley. There is an abundance of restaurants to choose from within the radius of a few blocks, and your host is an infallible source of tips on all manner of boutiques and antiques shops. The Orsay museum is minutes on foot and the Louvre not much farther across the river, but to satisfy a craving for incomparable Saint-Germain spirit you could limit your stay to meandering the streets of the 6th and 7th arrondissements and set off for home thoroughly sated.

BERTRAND PLASMANS'S COUPS DE COEUR

FLORIST AND GOURMET CONVENIENCE STORE
OLIVIER PITOU
14 and 22, rue des Saints-Pères, 75006
Tel.: 01 49 27 97 49 and 01 42 96 90 02
A stylish florist that also stocks balcony and terrace shrubs. Plasmans
commends Pitou's quality and originality. Down the street at 22, Pitou
has diversified his services with l'Épicerie, a gourmet convenience
store with delicious takeout.

BOUTIQUE—MENSWEAR
WICKET
11 bis, rue Chomel, 75007
Tel.: 01 44 39 95 50 | www.wicket.fr | wicketshop@wicket.fr
Tuesday–Saturday, 10:30 A.M.–7:00 P.M.
Hugues de Peyrelongue favors "le look British," which, interpreted by a
Frenchman with taste and flair, is a winning style. The bespoke suits,
jackets, and sportswear are good value.

ANTIQUES
GÉRARD MONLUC
14, rue des Saints-Pères, 76006
Tel.: 01 42 96 18 19 | gerardmonluc@wanadoo.fr
An elegant selection of eighteenth- and nineteenth-century furniture
and decorative arts you can be assured are authentic.

BOOKSTORE
LIBRAIRIE ALAIN KOGAN
15, rue du Bac, 75007
Tel.: 01 47 83 64 41
Independent bookseller where Plasmans picks up art books and Paris
guides for guests to peruse.

RESTAURANT
LE VOLTAIRE
27, Quai Voltaire, 75007
Tel.: 08 99 69 07 03
A sentimental choice, "for the timeless coté bourgeois atmosphere,
wood paneling, and authentic French cuisine, that has altered little
in the more than sixty years it has been in business."

WINDSOR HOME

High-style retro

Frédéric Barazer
3, rue Vital
750016 Paris
www.windsorhomeparis.fr

OPPOSITE:
Breakfast can be taken in
the ground floor sitting
room or adjoining interior
courtyard.

*P*LOTTING A ROMANTIC ASSIGNATION? Skip the cool-hunter haunts and opt for an eclectic gem in the heart of Establishment 16th. Windsor Home is not what you expect to find on a quiet cross street of this posh enclave above rue de Passy, a shopping artery thronged with faultlessly groomed women and *jeunesse dorée* texting on cell phones.

The BCBG character of the neighborhood lends a subversive edge to this bohemian guest house slotted sideways into the street behind an iron rail fence entwined with ivy. At first glance conservative—a niche in the facade is adorned with a classical vase, and the leafy garden courtyard is set with wrought-iron café tables and chairs—once inside the veneer of convention is pierced. The graphic motif of black-and-cream cement floor tiles is replicated in trompe-l'oeil wainscoting, and the stairwell is carpeted with a vivid purple runner edged in black, a funky melding of old and new that gives Windsor Home its one-of-a-kind flair.

Room décor ranges from the soothing lavender gray neoclassicism of room 4, with its lovely courtyard view, to the drama of Empire-themed room 8, overlooking rue Vital. Spacious room 8 is a symphony of intense red from cinnabar to ruby. A *méridienne* draped with a leopard skin redolent of an Ingres painting is juxtaposed with modernist brass bedside lamps, a minimalist art print above the bed, and a startling hot-pink WC.

Two suite-proportioned rooms off the entry hall are popular with long-stay guests as much for their high ceilings filigreed with creamy molding, chimneys, and ample light as for the privacy dividend of being able to slip in and out the building unnoticed. The daffodil-yellow walls of room 2 are paired with rich mauve drapes and black lacquer Louis-Philippe furniture. Timid it isn't, but the theatricality doesn't veer beyond the limit of taste; surreal details like bathroom sinks with pedestals resting on sculpted feet and pop lighting fixtures keep the mood playful.

You share the premises with youthful director Frédéric Barazer, whose family purchased the hotel in 2005 from Eric Chaillou—a decorator with an estate sale business who skillfully refurbished the hotel in 2003 but lacked the hotel management experience to leverage his design project into a viable service business.

OPPOSITE,
CLOCKWISE FROM TOP LEFT:
Bedroom decorated in a
lively neo-pop palette

Set back in a verdant
courtyard sideways to the
street, Windsor Home has
the discreet charm of a
private townhouse.

Bed reflected in fireplace
mirror, room 8.

Stylishly coordinated
decorative painting
adorns the cement floor
tiles, wainscoting, and
guest-room doors in the
ground-floor entry hall.

Raised in the hospitality and restaurant milieu, Frédéric immediately recognized the hotel's untapped potential. He describes his first visit posing as a potential guest as a *coup de foudre.*

Through hands-on management and select promotion, Frédéric has developed a loyal clientele he characterizes as "a pleasant mix, not a specific profile; everyone finds a place here—the eclectic décor seems to encourage variety." Because rates are reasonable and space limited, regulars are reluctant to share the address. Boutique hotels like to position themselves as homes away from home, but when twenty people are in residence it's often hard to sustain the domestic illusion. Windsor Home pulls it off with its hybrid ambiance of artsy boarding-house and elite group share. Managed by an owner who lives on the premises and gives guests his cell phone number if they need to reach him when he's out, the hotel offers a real sense of staying at someone's home.

Among Windsor Home's winning attributes are informality and absence of commercial infrastructure. Guests punch a code to get in and collect their tasseled room key from a key cubby under the staircase. Breakfast can be taken in one's room or in a small ground-floor sitting room. Maid service is minimally invasive, and guests are known to opt out when they sleep in.

Frédéric is passionate about quality food and wine, so be sure to seek his recommendations for dining out. Like many cultured Frenchmen, he savors authenticity and good value and is delighted to suggest itineraries for getting the most from your visit. If you are in the mood to hang out, sample a vintage from his well-referenced cave, which includes bottles from the family owned vineyard.

Don't miss a stroll down rue de Passy with a visit to fashion department store Franck et Fils at number 80, where customers are locals not tourists. Or find a table at an outdoor café and soak up the street life of a Parisian neighborhood that remains a holdout against homogeneity.

FRÉDÉRIC BARAZER'S COUPS DE COEUR

THEATER
THÉÂTRE NATIONAL DE CHAILLOT
1, place du Trocadéro, 75116

Tel.: 01 53 65 30 00 | www.theatre-chaillot.fr

Under the direction of Ariel Goldenberg, the three performance spaces showcase an eclectic program of classical music, dance, theater, and even circus and tango by established and emerging international artists and companies.

MUSEUM
PALAIS DU CHAILLOT
Cité de l'Architecture et du Patrimoine

1, place du Trocadéro, 75116

Tel.: 01 58 51 52 00

An art deco complex built in 1937 for the last Paris colonial exhibition at a time when France was the world's second colonial empire. A new center for architecture and patrimony was opened here in 2007 with an educational mission. Fascinating permanent collection, plus conferences and temporary exhibitions.

GOURMET FOOD—CHOCOLATE
PATRICK ROGER
45, avenue Victor Hugo, 75116

Tel.: 01 45 01 66 71 | www.patrickroger.com

Monday–Friday, 11:00 A.M.–7:30 P.M.; Saturday, 10:30 A.M.–7:30 P.M.

With just two shops in Paris, this Meilleur Ouvrier de France has yet to become a household name, but the distinctive mint packaging is instantly recognizable to connoisseurs. The fanciful window displays are worth a look.

RESTAURANT
LA MARÉE PASSY
71, avenue Paul Doumer, 75016

Tel.: 01 45 04 12 81 | www.lamareepassy.com

Open daily.

A chic but unpretentious fish and seafood restaurant with a blackboard menu featuring fresh catch, delivered daily. Best fish in the 16th, served in a contemporary nautical environment, where red replaces traditional blue as the signature color. Book ahead.

RESTAURANT
LE SCHEFFER
22, rue Scheffer, 75016

Tel.: 01 47 27 81 11

Traditional brasserie-bistro with retro décor, pleasant atmosphere, reliable cuisine, and *bon rapport qualité-prix* (good value).

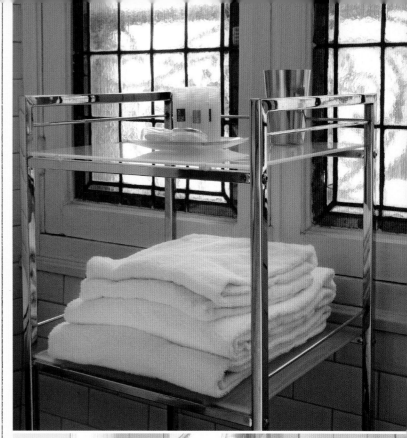

OPPOSITE, CLOCKWISE FROM TOP LEFT:
Detail of glass inlay mural, dining room of Daniel.

Detail of embossed leather mural, Oscar Wilde Suite at L'Hôtel.

Bath tiled in Moroccan zelig, Villa d'Estrée.

Boudoir

LE DANIEL
(8th), *Champs-Élysées*
Four-star fantasia

L'HÔTEL
(6th), *Beaux-Arts*
Romantic baroque

VILLA D'ESTRÉE
(6th), *Saint-Michel*
Latin Quarter for lovers

If you are seeking a romantic interlude in sensuous surroundings redolent with history and exoticism, a boudoir hotel should satisfy your needs. Sensitive to the desire for privacy and independence, these three hotels have created sitting room and salon spaces or generous suite-style guest rooms tailor-made for tête-à-tête conversations or discreet assignations.

Jacques Garcia, master of baroque boudoir style, designed the lavish interiors for l'Hôtel, which ranks among the world's premier small hotels, and a Garcia-trained designer is responsible for the richly textured, more intimate Villa d'Estrée.

The Daniel is the most exotic Parisian hideaway, yet embodies a distinctly Parisian sensibility, incorporating influences of French colonial history. Owned and designed by women, it is unusually rich in decorative detail, with attention paid to quality and comfort in every domain.

LE DANIEL

Four-star fantasia

Nammour family
8, rue Frédéric Bastiat
75008 Paris
www.hoteldanielparis.com

OPPOSITE:
Daniel's pan-Oriental
décor features Chinese
porcelain, custom-painted
de Gournay wallpaper,
and Lebanese tableware.

*T*HE DANIEL IS A TWO-FOR-ONE escapist retreat offering the seclusion of a tranquil location in the midst of a lively neighborhood plus immersion in a lavish East-meets-West interior created by designer Tarfa Salam.

Conveniently nested between the Champs-Élysées and Faubourg Saint-Honoré, the hotel's Haussmann facade, with wrought-iron marquee and lanterns, appears classic enough. Only flowering potted camellias hint at the exotic beauty and refinement within. Ignoring a minimalist trend in hotel design, the Daniel is a treasure trove of unabashed ornamentation. The designer's brief was to create an evocative cross-cultural haven where fantasy and nostalgia coalesce within a very Parisian context—an ambiance that reflects the heritage and globetrotting lifestyle of the owners. No expense was spared in the fulfillment of the owners' vision. The quality of materials and craftsmanship is outstanding, and there isn't a false note in color choice or fabric selection.

Salam, based in London, tapped myriad sources including French period décor inspired by Middle and Far Eastern vernacular. Several artists were commissioned to create original pieces. Gerard Coltat's shimmering exotic garden-themed murals crafted of encrusted glass transform the dining room into an enchanted kingdom.

The proprietors are avid collectors, and their finds are focal points of the décor. A jewel-tone stem glass collection fills a display case covering the wall above the sky-lit dining banquette; in the entry a carpet from Kazakhstan, eighteenth-century Chinese plates, and mother-of-pearl–encrusted Syrian end tables are complemented by a classic George Smith custom-upholstered English sofa.

The sophistication of Salam's eye is evident in a juggling of disparate styles and a harmonious medley of texture and pattern. The effect is rich yet reposeful, with a dose of levity to keep it from veering into kitsch or conceptual. The salon is delightfully comfortable, and guests are encouraged to make it their own. Breakfast pastries are set out in the morning, replaced by cake and biscuits at teatime. Cocktails are served from the ornate bar throughout the day and evening.

Almond green is a signature shade and is especially effective as background on hand-painted eighteenth-century-style de Gournay wallpaper designed in

ABOVE, FROM LEFT:

Hammered metal sink inset within a white marble counter.

Marquetry backgammon tables, salon.

Detail, ornate mirror inlaid with mother of pearl, suite 501.

OPPOSITE:

Salon arranged in conversational groupings features inlaid Middle-Eastern furnishings, shimmering silk, and Chinese decorative objects.

China. The ebony-and-pearl–inlaid marquetry tables were designed by Nada Debs. Matching sets of armchairs are paired with tables inlaid with backgammon boards, which double as dining tables when the adjoining restaurant fills up.

The restaurant is a popular neighborhood draw and is fully booked for lunch weekdays. Denis Fetisson, a talented thirty-year-old chef who began his career at fourteen in the kitchen of an uncle's restaurant in the Midi, maintains an allegiance to the produce and clear flavors of Provence despite stints at restaurants in Cannes, Mexico City, Courchevel, and London. Fetisson describes his cuisine as "a contemporary interpretation of a classic heritage." His dishes incorporate elements of Asian and Middle Eastern cuisine, but he confides that a chef's predilections are established early on and having grown up on the Mediterranean he considers fish more "noble" than meat.

Asian motifs predominate in guest rooms featuring historic toile de Jouy prints—Siam from Manuel Canovas, Voyage of Marco Polo from Schumacher, Kipling from Nobilis, and Cairo Fair from Lee Jofa. Leaving the ground floor, the color palette is more subdued, with chalky green, silvery taupe, and powdery pink fabrics and neutral carpeting. Bathrooms match the luxurious standard of the establishment and are appointed with Moroccan zellig and marble. In keeping with the occidental/oriental theme, the toiletry selection includes Dead Sea bath salts and Molton Brown of London products. As is customary in nineteenth-century Parisian buildings, front rooms on the second and fifth floors have balconies shaded by retractable canvas awnings, permitting guests to enjoy breakfast or a drink alfresco.

LEFT:
A collection of jewel-tone
stemware is on display
above the plush dining-
room banquette.

OPPOSITE:
Decorative mother-of-
pearl-inlaid mirror and
commodes complement
restrained elegance of a
George Smith custom-
upholstered sofa in a
spacious suite.

NOUR DEMARQUETTE'S COUPS DE COEUR

MUSEUM
MUSÉE JACQUEMART ANDRÉ

158, boulevard Haussmann, 75008
Tel.: 01 45 62 11 59 | message@musee-jacquemart-andre.com
Open daily, 10:00 A.M.–6:00 P.M.
The capital's premier private art collection is housed in the former nineteenth-century mansion of banker Edouard André and his artist wife, Nelie Jacquemart. Their exceptional collection of Flemish, eighteenth-century French, and Italian Renaissance paintings and rare furniture is supplemented by temporary exhibitions. Lovely tea salon.

RESTAURANT
APICIUS

20, rue d'Artois, 75008
Tel.: 01 43 80 19 66 | restaurant-apicius@wanadoo.fr
Twenty yards from the hotel in a private mansion surrounded by a lovely garden, Chef Jean-Pierre Vigato's Michelin two-star restaurant is an enchanted setting for a gastronomic treat.

HEALTH AND BEAUTY
ESPACE PAYOT

62, rue Pierre Charron, 75008
Tel.: 01 45 61 42 08 | www.payot.com
The Daniel has a close relationship with this high-design beauty and fitness center with a stunning swimming pool and every creature comfort. Complete range of massages and Payot beauty treatments.

GOURMET FOOD—BAKERY
BOULANGERIE KAYSER

85, boulevard Malsherbes, 75008
Tel.: 01 45 22 70 33
Monday–Saturday, 7:00 A.M.–8:30 P.M.
Eric Kayser traveled the world training bakers before opening his first shop, on rue Monge. This branch is also a restaurant. Outstanding breakfast pastries and sandwiches.

BOUTIQUE—ASIAN DECORATIVE OBJECTS
COMPAGNIE FRANCAISE DE L'ORIENT ET DE LA CHINE

170, boulevard Haussmann, 75008
Tel.: 01 53 53 40 80
In keeping with the hotel's Asiatic spirit, a selection of decorative objects, handcrafts, jewelry, and antiques from China and the rest of Asia.

L'HÔTEL

Romantic baroque

Peter Frankopan
13, rue des Beaux-Arts
75006 Paris
www.l-hotel.com

*I*F YOU HAD TO PICK the sexiest hotel in Paris, this would be it. Location, legend, décor, and candlelit subterranean pool for two all conspire to seduce. As if that weren't enough, Michelin just awarded the hotel's romantic winter garden restaurant its first star.

Unassumingly situated on a street of established galleries between the Seine and place Saint-Germain-des-Prés, the 1816 Directoire facade belies an opulent interior fashioned by celebrity decorator Jacques Garcia. The ground floor is a sequence of alternating light and dark plush nooks leading back through bar to sitting room to light-filled restaurant.

Garcia's flamboyant remix of historic styles (with a predilection for Empire and 1900) favors trompe l'oeil marble, neo-Roman frescoes, black lacquer, gilt, and jewel-tone pleated and tasseled upholstering strewn with cushions. A soupçon of decadence pays homage to the hotel's reputation as a refuge for clandestine lovers and intellectual bohemians.

The most spectacular architectural feature is a six-story atrium rotunda with domed skylight illuminating a classical black-and-white marble floor. Twenty guest rooms ranging in proportion from the intimate Boudoir to top-floor Cardinal Suite with terrace are decorated according to historical or stylistic themes—from King of Naples, Pondicherry, and Marco Polo, to Oscar Wilde. A jewel-box elevator quilted in blue velvet lets out onto corridors wrapped around the central atrium, with its graceful arches and terra-cotta Roman medallions. Purple panther-motif carpet and flickering wall sconces add to the aura of fantasy.

None of the illustrious guests has eclipsed Oscar Wilde, who spent his final year at what was then Hôtel d'Alsace. Shortly before breathing his last in room 16 on November 30, 1900, he treated friends to a final immortal quote, "My wallpaper and I are fighting a duel to the death. One or other of us has got to go." More than a century later, Wilde would be pleased that his legacy of theatrical nonconformity lives on. Room 16 is consecrated to his memory with framed correspondence, photos, and cartoon sketches. Décor is a luxe French interpretation of Victorian arts and crafts, and the sumptuous peacock-themed painted leather walls would elicit a memorable quip from their inspiration.

Another shrine to a legendary guest is room 36, favored by French music-hall diva Mistinguette. The hotel acquired some of her furnishings, including a

OPPOSITE:
Guest rooms give onto a
central atrium rotunda
adorned with classical
medallions.

40

ABOVE, FROM LEFT:
Art deco clock and period Lalique crystal dish, Mistinguette room.

Period Oscar Wilde caricature

A canopied bed reflected in the mantle mirror of a quiet "chic" category room overlooking the rear courtyard.

OPPOSITE TOP:
The Minstinguette room is funished with the musical hall diva's own art deco bedroom suite.

OPPOSITE BOTTOM LEFT:
Marco Polo suite with elaborately carved Chinese furniture and pair of oversize porcelain vases.

OPPOSITE BOTTOM RIGHT:
Bedroom, Cardinal apartment with terrace.

fabulous deco-mirrored bed. *Galucha* (stingray) wall covering, peach drapes, chrome hardware, and Lalique frosted-glass sconces create an ambiance to rival a Hollywood movie set.

Bathrooms are given equal attention with lavish marble, deep tubs, and retro fixtures. The Marco Polo room deserves special mention for beautiful Chinese Silk Road décor. For the ultimate in relaxing soaks, guests can book the private dipping pool and *hammam*, or Turkish bath. The blue mosaic-tile pool is shaped to the contours of the antique cellar with impressive vaulted stone ceiling. Votive candles rim the pool's edge to heighten the romance of the setting.

The kitchen at the hotel is run by the ambitious young chef Philippe Bélissent, who trained at three-star Ledoyen before coming to l'Hôtel in 2005. His light-handed and inventive seasonal cuisine is garnering considerable praise. The astutely edited *carte* includes a popular lunch special menu that is quite affordable.

The hotel's immediate neighborhood has one of the best selections of restaurants, cafés, boutiques, and galleries in the city and is enjoyable to wander on foot. As for cultural exclusivity, l'Hotel is a block from both the École des Beaux-Arts and Institute of France, gathering place of forty living "Immortals": writers, scientists, philosophers, and statesmen who make up the French Academy, the country's oldest and most august institution.

If you don't check into l'Hotel in the mood for romance, it shouldn't take long to succumb to the seduction of this mythical destination.

BOUTIQUE—JEWELRY
MARIE-HÉLÈNE DE TAILLAC

8, rue de Tournon, 75006

Tel.: 01 44 27 07 07 | www.mariehelenedetaillac.com

Monday–Saturday.

De Taillac's design philosophy challenges the conventional notion of precious stones and "serious" jewelry. Creative experience with prestige fashion and design houses helped her "set stones free" from heavy, formal settings. Her light, fanciful collection is crafted in India by master jewelers. Brightly colored gems and delicately worked eighteen-karat gold are her signature materials.

GALLERY
GALERIE CLAUDE BERNARD

7–9, rue des Beaux-Arts, 75006

Tel.: 01 43 26 97 07 | www.claude-bernard.com

Tuesday–Saturday.

Forty-year veteran of the Paris gallery world Claude Bernard sets the blue-chip standard for contemporary figuration. The annual show schedule includes six exhibitions of living artists interspersed with modern masters from Bacon and Morandi to Cartier-Bresson.

MUSEUM
MUSÉE DELACROIX

6, rue de Furstenberg, 75006

Tel.: 01 44 41 86 50 | www.musee-delacroix.fr

Open daily, 9:30 A.M.–5 P.M.; closed Tuesday.

Residence and garden-level studio where the great Romantic painter spent his six final years. Delacroix moved here to facilitate completion of a commission at nearby Église Saint-Sulpice. Personal effects and his inimitable sketchbooks are highlights.

RESTAURANT—VEGETARIAN CUISINE AND HEALTH FOOD STORE
GUENMAÏ

Corner of 6, rue Cardinale and 2 bis, rue de l'Abbaye, 75006

Tel.: 01 43 26 03 24

Fashion world address for a stringently healthful yet delicious lunch you'd never guess existed in the land of foie gras and Camembert. The dining room is an annex to a natural food and supplements boutique.

INTERIOR DESIGN—PRESTIGE FABRIC HOUSES
PLACE DE FURSTENBERG, 75006

This romantic square is the epicenter of fine home furnishing fabric collections. Canovas, Pierre Frey, Lelievre, and Braquenié, to cite a few, keep company with antiques shops, chic clothing boutiques, and the neighborhood's long-established booksellers.

VILLA D'ESTRÉE

Latin Quarter for lovers

Chevance family
17, rue Gît-le-Coeur
75006 Paris
www.vilaadestrees.com

OPPOSITE:
Suite with exposed beams
in the "Residence des
Arts" annex, where each
room is equipped with a
galley kitchen.

FEW SECTIONS OF PARIS match a visitor's idealized expectation as satisfyingly as the maze of narrow streets crisscrossing the northeast corner of the 6th arrondissement bordered by the Seine and boulevard Saint-Michel. The concentration of history is palpable, and it's hard to walk more than a few meters without admiring the facade of a beautifully restored *hôtel particulier* or being tempted to pause at a sidewalk café and savor the ambiance.

Wandering up toward the Seine you might come upon Villa d'Estrée, tucked into sleepy rue Gît-le-Coeur, which spans the quay and rue Saint André des Arts, a street crammed with restaurants, art cinemas, and shops. The hotel complex is something of a village within a village, comprising two small buildings on opposite sides of the street and a retro bistro on the corner of Saint-André-des-Arts. The hotel is named for Gabrielle d'Estrée, mistress of Henri IV, who is believed to have resided on Gît-le-Coeur—which, though it sounds romantic, is the name of a historic chef.

Yann and Laetitia Chevance, the youthful brother-sister team running the show, bring to their roles precious savoir-faire gained in a family business plus the international perspective of an American MBA. Yann is the public face of the duo and an excellent source of insider tips that will add to the enjoyment of your stay. Being married to a New Yorker, he is more than sympathetic to the minor stresses of adapting to a foreign culture. His friendly informality encourages guests with the inclination to establish a rapport. "When people open up to us we are ready to help them with anything" is how Yann characterizes the hospitality at Villa d'Estrée.

The hotel's principal building has ten spacious rooms set up two per floor and an elegant boudoir-style ground-level salon with plenty of comfortable seating, where breakfast is served. The scale and services correspond to a luxurious bed-and-breakfast for travelers who appreciate low-key sophistication and tranquility. The receptionist, who by virtue of not having scores of people to look after is able to respond quickly to client needs, buzzes guests in. Through word of mouth, the hotel is popular with newlyweds who relish the luxury of anonymity and unscheduled time.

Interior designer Yani Decamps, who trained with star hotel decorator Jacques Garcia (whose work at über-trendy Hotel Costes sparked a wave of imitation), has borrowed from his mentor's stylebook with enough originality to keep it

Guestrooms feature
comfortable sitting areas.

Room overlooking art
house cinema Saint
André des Arts.

Designer Yani Decamps
incorporates eclectic
decorative touches such
as Japanese wood-block
prints within a neoclassic
theme.

Detail, guest room sitting
area with reproduction
period wall covering.

fresh. The historic and geographic connotations of the names Villa d'Estrée and Café Latin on the corner, are likely inspiration for Decamps's contemporary interpretation of Empire décor replete with appropriation of Roman motifs. The color register and fabrics are rich, and furnishings include low striped silk-and-velvet-upholstered couches and armchairs, ebony wood furniture with gilt trim, fringed lampshades, and Persian carpet. Low lighting and mauve walls give the room just the right note of bohemian baroque.

Guest-room interiors are individualized, which makes picking a favorite tricky: each has lovely details and appealing character to recommend it—whether it be a series of Japanese wood-block prints or built-in shelves at bedside stocked with guide books. All guest rooms benefit from windows overlooking the charming street with a handsomely restored historic residence directly opposite. Every guest room has a desk and plenty of seating. Having two rooms per floor is a useful layout for families or groups of friends who wish to enjoy the privacy of their own apartment. The most dramatic elements are the bathrooms, several of which are tiled in glossy black or a pattern of terra-cotta-and-cream Moroccan zellig tiles. Toiletries are customized for the hotel.

The hotel's second building, referred to as the "Résidence des Arts," offers a self-service alternative. Rooms include a small kitchenette, and guests let themselves in with a front-door key. There are several suites, and décor is equally attractive but there is no receptionist or salon. Excellent for long-term visits and families with children or those who prefer the flexibility of preparing their own meals.

The bonus resource for visitors to either side of the street is Café Latin, which has all the makings of a dream canteen. Nostalgic mustard-colored walls, tile floor, tin advertisements, vintage posters, and bentwood chairs set the stage for a convivial meal. It's open year round late morning till midnight seven days a week, so guests are never in danger of going hungry. A blackboard posted outside announces specials, and the menu proposes standards such as *soupe à l'oignon gratinée*, steak tartare, *poulet fermier roti*, and *tarte Tatin*. Chef Pierre, after a dozen years in the kitchen, knows his customers and doesn't hesitate to please with rib-sticking classics like *choucroute paysanne* and *coq au vin,* incorporating the influence of his native Vendée.

The wine list features a pleasing range of *vins du propriétaire,* most of which are available by the glass or pitcher, and it is hard to imagine a more welcoming destination for a glass of red at sunset.

RESTAURANT
CASA BINI

36, rue Grégoire de Tours, 75006
Tel.: 01 46 34 05 60
Monday–Saturday lunch and dinner; Sunday dinner.
Anna Bini opened her native Tuscan-inspired restaurant twenty years ago and continues to impress with the freshness and sincerity of her cooking. Carpaccio is a staple, along with daily pasta specials.

RESTAURANT
LE CHRISTINE

1, rue Christine, 75006
Tel.: 01 40 51 71 54
Daily, 6:30 P.M.–midnight; closed Sunday.
The intimate dining room overlooking a courtyard in a historic residence exudes classic Saint-Germain charm. Recently restored by a genial couple with a penchant for traditional cuisine. The fixed-price menu is good value.

GOURMET FOOD —TEA
MARRIAGE FRÈRES

Rue des Grands-Augustins, 75006
Tel.: 01 40 51 82 50
Open daily. Shop and museum: 10:30 A.M.–7:30 P.M.
Tea restaurant: 12–3 P.M. Tea salon: 3–7 P.M.
Founded in 1854 and classed among the world's finest tea merchants. New blends are introduced every year. Their best endorsement is that the number of outlets in Japan is higher than in France. The charming boutique is stocked floor to ceiling with canisters and teapots of every description.

LANDMARK
PONT NEUF BY NIGHT, 75006

The "new" bridge, which recently celebrated its four-hundredth anniversary, is now the oldest bridge spanning the Seine. Built by Henry IV as a series of arches in two spans meeting in the middle at the tip of the Île de la Cité. Modern for its day, it was the first bridge in the city without residential buildings and had a sidewalk to protect pedestrians from mud splashed by passing horses and carts.

PARK
LUXEMBOURG GARDENS, 75006

The most elegant of Parisian parks is a seven-minute walk from the hotel. Great for jogging or strolling down the tree-lined allées and around the basin in front of the Luxembourg Palace, which houses the national senate. Pull up one of the metal chairs for a rest, as sitting on the lawns is not permitted.

OPPOSITE, CLOCKWISE FROM TOP LEFT:

Detail, Eiffel tower suite, Dokhans.

Coffee served in winter garden, Keppler.

Detail, Circular booth, Sezz bar.

Bannister, Le Placide.

Design classics

DOKHAN'S
(16th), Trocadéro
Clubhouse for connoisseurs

KEPPLER
(16th), Avenue Marceau
Graphic urbane glamour

SEZZ
(16th), Passy
Contemporary enclave with an exclusive aura

LE PLACIDE
(6th), Sèvres-Babylone
Luxe, calme, et lucidité

In the conception of a Design Classics hotel, no aesthetic decision is left to chance. From the placement of a bibelot on a salon side table to the scent of a fragrant candle, every element contributes to the harmony of the whole. Design Classics represent the work of France's finest interior architects, chosen by hotel proprietors for their ability to create unique environments that enhance the architectural qualities of the site while expressing the taste and character of the owner.

These destinations share a high level of sophistication and style. Placide and Sezz are contemporary and streamlined, complemented by an atmosphere of informality that softens the impact of design rigor. Dokhan's pays homage to the grace and refinement of French eighteenth- and nineteenth-century period furnishings and has some lovely works of art, while Keppler is a high-gloss symphony in urbane black-and-white. Pack a note pad. You'll want to jot down ideas that could translate nicely *chez vous*.

DOKHAN'S

Clubhouse for connoisseurs

Dokhan family
117, rue Lauriston
75116 Paris
website to come

OPPOSITE:
Canopied bed nestled
in semi-circular niche,
top-floor Ming Suite.

*Y*OU MAY WONDER, Why the name Dokhan's? Paris hotels tend to take their name from a monument, historic personage, design motif, or location, but Dohkan's is none of these. The answer makes perfect sense when you discover that the hotel is a made-to-measure commission of the Dokhan family. Their brief to fashionable Parisian decorator Frédéric Méchiche was to create a discreetly sumptuous *demure privée*, enhancing the building's neoclassical style with the patina of noble recuperated materials and the restraint of contemporary design.

The wedge-shaped 1910 Palladian-style mansion sits like a miniature Flatiron at the apex of rues Lauriston and Didier. Snappy black-and-white striped awnings shade the corner entrance and ground-floor windows—a clubby motif reinforced by clipped boxwoods flanking the entrance and window boxes with ivy-covered trellises.

The entry-hall rotunda is in the spirit of a winter garden. Silk balloon shades and a pair of velvet upholstered Directoire settees in deep emerald complement glossy white pilasters and an antique marble checkerboard floor. Topiary boxwoods in black pots complete the effect.

The Dokhan family engaged Méchiche, their personal interior architect, to collaborate on this haute couture project, for his cultured eye and sensitivity to craftsmanship and fine art. The ground-floor salons are rich with treasures recovered from historic properties, which give the hotel an unusual degree of character. The parquet flooring originated in a chateau, and the exquisite gilded celadon *boiseries* of the Champagne bar are original eighteenth century. Even the elevator paneled with the leather and wood of a reassembled 1930s Louis Vuitton trunk, is imaginatively customized.

The elegant double salon is a Parisian interpretation of English Georgian style. Marble busts top polished wood pedestals and mauve-gray walls are given a Wedgwood treatment with white trim and low-relief Roman emblems. A Georgian fireplace, gilt-edged black lacquer Regency-style and slipper chairs upholstered in striped black-and-cream moiré further a mood of neoclassical formalism. Engravings by Matisse and Picasso, an eighteenth-century Italian console table, and seventeenth-century pastoral paintings provide the right counterpoints of eclecticism and warmth.

OPPOSITE TOP LEFT:
Stairwell alcove,
Eiffel apartment.

OPPOSITE BOTTOM LEFT:
Salon fireplace,
Eiffel apartment.

OPPOSITE RIGHT:
The wedge-shaped
former mansion built
in 1910 recalls New York's
Flatiron building of
the same epoch.

OVERLEAF,
TOP AND BOTTOM RIGHT:
Details, champagne bar.

Throughout the hotel Méchiche's signature stripes are reprised in myriad variations on handpainted and upholstered walls, couches, and cushions. In guest rooms they are coordinated with tone-on-tone floral printed fabrics and carpeting for a cozy ambiance, and the graphic palette is softened with china blue and periwinkle. Mahogany- or ebony-hued Empire and Regency furniture and gilded black metal lighting fixtures predominate. A more contemporary mood reigns in the top-floor Eiffel apartment with sisal carpeting, bamboo roll shades, and stripped natural wood fireplace and paneling. With its intimate view of the Eiffel Tower from the sitting room and fully equipped bar, the apartment suite convincingly replicates a pied-à-terre.

The décor of each guest room is different and personalized with antique mirrors, engravings, and bibelots. Many of the rooms have romantic chintz canopies suspended around the headboard and the mood, while impressively elegant, is always comfy and reposeful. The marble and mirrored bathrooms are impeccable.

The jewel of the hotel is the eighteenth-century-inspired dining room paneled in antique *boiseries* adorned with pilasters, gilded molding, period mirrors, and decorative panels painted with Renaissance motifs. The dining room is transformed at twilight into an ultra romantic candle-lit Champagne bar. With a cellar of over fifty vintages, it is considered the city's premier Champagne bar, and youthful sommelier Mikael's hospitality and knowledge have engendered a devoted clientele of connoisseurs and amateurs.

Mikael is a fervent promoter of Champagne's unheralded complexity. His mission is to educate the palette and develop an appreciation for the charm of demibruts and natural vinification. Encouraged by the response to his weekly tasting selections of three vintages, Mikael has also organized thematic events such as an introduction to eighteenth-century vinification techniques being revived by select Champagne houses. The bar offers a light menu to complement the personality of featured *cépages*.

Dokhan's location in the northeast section of the 16th arrondissement is conveniently situated between Trocadero and avenue Georges V and the Champs-Élysées in the neighboring 8th arrondissement. The Left Bank is also readily accessible. This end of the 16th has the benefit of being less hectic than the more commercial 8th, yet is not as sleepily residential as the southwest end of the arrondissement. Dokhan's is a low-key luxury retreat of rare tranquility with a standard of service to match flashier competition.

LUXURY HOTELS ASIA/PACIFIC

AFRICA Michael Poliza

DOKHAN FAMILY'S COUP DE COEURS

RESTAURANT
LA TABLE LAURISTON
129, rue Lauriston, 75016
Tel.: 01 47 27 00 07
Welcome traditional bistro in a *quartier* linked with gastronomic grandeur. The décor is bright contemporary, but the menu is grounded in regional classics and specials tied to fresh seasonal produce.

RESTAURANT
CAFÉ DE L'HOMME
Musée de l'Homme
17, place du Trocadéro, 75116
Tel.: 01 44 05 30 15 | www.restaurant-cafedelhomme.com
One of the most elegant and unexpected contemporary restaurant spaces in the city with a fabulous panoramic view (especially from the terrace) down terraced esplanades leading to the Seine and across to the Eiffel Tower.

GOURMET—CAFÉ, CULINARY BOUTIQUE, AND COOKING SCHOOL
LENÔTRE
48, avenue Victor Hugo, 75116
Tel.: 01 45 02 21 21 | www.lenotre.fr
Parisian showcase of the French ambassador of gastronomy. The Belle Époque pavilion includes a café with outdoor terrace, gourmet food, and culinary gift shop, cooking school, and reception rooms for catered events.

RESTAURANT
THE CRISTAL ROOM–BACCARAT
11, place des États-Unis, 75116
Tel.: 01 40 22 11 10 | www.baccarat.com
Monday–Saturday, 12:30 P.M.–5 P.M.
Philippe Starck's transformation of Marie-Laure de Noailles's former dining room combines refinement and rusticity, juxtaposing an astonishing baroque crystal chandelier and gilded stucco with raw brick walls. Chef Thierry Burlot's versatile menu accommodates the gamut of taste and appetite.

MUSEUM
MUSÉE D'ART MODERNE DE LA VILLE DE PARIS
11, avenue du Président Wilson, 75116
Tel.: 01 53 67 40 80
Tuesday–Sunday, 10 A.M.–6 P.M. Closed Mondays and certain holidays. Filling the gaps between the d'Orsay and the Beaubourg, with a rich collection covering major movements from Fauvism to contemporary video artists. A thorough education in French modernism and late-century art.

KEPPLER

Graphic urbane glamour

Nouvel family
10, rue Keppler
75016 Paris
www.keppler.fr

THE KEPPLER IS THE NEWEST ADDITION to the Nouvel family Parisian Hotel Collection, a diverse group of five boutique hotels split between Saint-Germain and the Champs-Élysées. To attain the standard of prior acquisitions, the Keppler underwent a total transformation, reemerging as the most glamorous new Parisian four-star of 2007. Designer Pierre Yves Rochon broke with his Georges V bourgeois-chic register and injected plenty of pizzazz into this project. He succeeded in creating a contemporary environment while eschewing a trend for modernist minimalism. There is a high level of creature comfort throughout and consistent use of top-quality fabrics, furniture, and fixtures. Black-and-white is the unifying theme expressed in multiple patterns— checkerboard marble flooring in the entry and central hall; zebra, candy cane, and pinstripes in the salon; and arabesque ceramics and chinoiserie rug in the atrium-ceiling winter garden.

On the ground floor, Rochon replicates the intimacy of a luxurious private residence, or at least one you might admire in the pages of *Architectural Digest*. There are decorative objects galore, with a partiality for exotic ginger jar vases, marquetry boxes, and animal imagery. Upholstered furniture in tweedy mixes of charcoal flecked with cream provides a cozy counterpoint to high-gloss detail.

The main salon is sumptuously appointed with a British-style mahogany bar and fireplace framed by bookcases stocked with a well-edited collection of culture and lifestyle titles. The sunny winter garden atrium has accordion-fold doors for more seclusion. In addition to being a quiet sitting room, tables and chairs make it a welcome spot to set up your computer, enjoy an afternoon tea, or order in a meal.

The décor of the breakfast room is softer. A wall above the row of fern-green banquettes and elegant medallion-back chairs are upholstered in retro magnolia print fabric with a whiff of establishment Palm Beach. Despite a *sous sol* location, natural light channeled into a landscaped vitrine dispels any hint of enclosure. The zinc breakfast buffet in an adjoining alcove proposes a cornucopia of options consistent with an exceptional quality of service for a small hotel. The *table d'hôte* running down the center of the room is practical for large groups or a catered private meal. A fitness center on the lower level includes sauna and steam room facilities.

OPPOSITE:
Sunny winter
garden salon with
atrium glass ceiling.

ABOVE, FROM LEFT:
Taps within easy reach of a reclining bather, Jacuzzi tub.

The breakfast room is available for small catered parties.

Detail, magnolia print fabric, breakfast room.

OPPOSITE TOP LEFT:
Detail, trio of gymnast sculptures, winter garden salon.

OPPOSITE TOP RIGHT:
In guest rooms, sunny lemon-yellow accents soften the graphic rigor.

OPPOSITE BOTTOM:
Two-bedroom sixth-floor suite.

OVERLEAF:
Graphic black and white is the unifying theme expressed in multiple patterns.

The graphic bicolor scheme is carried over into guest rooms that are alternately accented with yellow, soft green, or mauve depending on size category. Furniture is black lacquer and the lighting is excellent. Bathrooms have black marble floors, and walls are covered either in Ralph Lauren striped wallpaper or black oilcloth.

Handsome red, brown, and black sixth-floor suites have the feel of luxurious penthouse apartments. Suite 602 with two bedrooms and baths is well suited for travel with children. Suite 601 has a spectacular terrace furnished with black metal furniture upholstered in pristine cream whipcord, where you can admire the Eiffel Tower while reclining on the chaise longue in the shade of electronically operated awnings.

Situated on the border of the 8th arrondissement, minutes from the Champs-Élysées, Arc de Triomphe, and avenue Georges V, rue Kepler is a tiny one-way street with a tranquil residential air. Once inside the felted comfort of the hotel, double-glazed windows, solid doors, and plush carpeting guarantee that you quickly forget you are in one of busiest sections of the city. The Kepler offers the buzz of being at the hub of action along with the comfort and hospitality of an exclusive private club.

FOUNDATION

FONDATION PIERRE BERGÉ – YVES SAINT LAURENT

1, rue Léonce Reynaud – 75116

Tel.: 01 44 31 64 00

Monday–Friday 9:00 A.M.–1:00 P.M. & 2:30 P.M.–6:00 P.M.

When Saint Laurent and Bergé closed YSL Couture in 2002, they converted their headquarters and couture ateliers into a museum, research library, and exhibition space. The collection includes 5,000 couture outfits, 15,000 accessories, sketches, personal mementos, and more.

GOURMET FOOD—CHOCOLATE

LA MAISON DU CHOCOLAT

52, rue François 1er, 75008

Tel.: 01 47 23 38 25

Monday–Saturday, 10 A.M.–7:30 P.M.

Robert Linxe, nicknamed "wizard of the ganache," opened the second boutique of his international empire here in 1987. The secret of his handmade creations is savoir faire—attributed to the finest ingredients, expert handling, and never using a higher grade than 65% pure cacao

RESTAURANT

LA MAISON BLANCHE

15, avenue Montaigne, 75008

Tel.: 01 47 23 55 99 | www.maison-blanche.fr

reservation@maison-blanche.fr

Perched in a minimalist cube atop the Théâtre des Champs-Élysées, with gorgeous views and décor to match. Inventive Languedoc cuisine from celebrated Pourcin twins, Jacques and Laurent.

RESTAURANT

FERMETTE MARBEUF 1900

5, rue Marbeuf, 75008

Tel.: 01 53 23 08 00 | www.fermettemarbeuf.com

Ask to be seated in the main winter garden room under the skylight—an art nouveau classic replete with hand-painted tiles. The traditional cuisine is inspired by seasonal produce, and the service is attentive and experienced.

BOUTIQUE—WOMEN'S FASHION AND ACCESSORIES

BALENCIAGA

10, avenue Georges V, 75008

Tel.: 01 47 20 21 11

Nicholas Ghesquière's visionary architectural creations with a hint of provocation revived the fortunes of a fashion house founded by the Spanish master. The futuristic flagship boutique sells ready-to-wear and accessories beloved of fashion icons Gwyneth Paltrow and Charlotte Gainsbourg.

SEZZ

Contemporary enclave
with an exclusive aura

Shahé Kalaidjian
6, avenue Frémiet
75016 Paris
www.hotelsezz.com

SEZZ EPITOMIZES THE NOTION of the confidential address. Even the name, a *jeu de mot* on its location (*seize* means "sixteen" in French), implies insider destination. The wordplay is emblematic of the nonconformist spirit of this unconventional but faultlessly elegant hotel.

It doesn't get much calmer than avenue Frémiet, which despite the grandiose connotations of the word *avenue* is a sleepy one-way block lined with art nouveau apartment buildings. Right off the quay in the shadow of Pont Bir-Hakeim, its location is deceptively remote. The Passy Métro stop is up a flight of steps around the corner and just down the quay; on opposite ends of Pont d'Iéna are Trocadéro and the Eiffel Tower.

Owner Shahé Kalaidjian flouts several hotel conventions at Sezz. The first is staff hierarchy. To avoid the frustrations of a "pass the buck" mentality he frequently encounters as a hotel guest, Kalaidjian compressed the chain of command. There are no concierges or baggage handlers. Instead, guests are assigned a PA (production assistant) whose job it is to look after their needs throughout their stay. The autonomy encourages resourcefulness and greater sensitivity to the expectations of guests.

Room layout likewise defies convention. Who says a bed has to be pushed up against a wall? Chez Sezz, high-design steel camp beds with low leather headboards are centerpieces. Ingenious pull-out drawers slide out from beneath the mattress in lieu of night tables, and bedtime reading is illuminated by a pair of rheostat-control glass vase- shaped lights posed on a slender desk behind the headboard. A glass wall separates the bedroom and bath. When every surface material is selected for its inherent beauty and sinks, tubs, and faucets are minimalist sculpture, there is nothing to hide. Ample closet space eliminates any excuse for clutter.

The pared-down, somewhat masculine interior is the work of Christophe Pillet, a multitalented designer as known for sophisticated product and furniture design as for commercial and private interior design projects. Much of the furniture is by Pillet, including comfortable molded plastic and steel faux-alligator-skin chairs.

Lighting design is both playful and sleek. Lampshades are banished, replaced

OPPOSITE:
Play of transparencies:
the view across the
entryway between
the ground-floor
sitting rooms.

OPPOSITE TOP:
Sleek camp-style beds are
positioned in the middle
of guest rooms.

OPPOSITE BOTTOM LEFT:
Bed and bath are
separated by a
glass wall.

OPPOSITE BOTTOM RIGHT:
A tub designed for two,
with pillow head rests at
either end to facilitate
conversation.

by suspended transparent tubular fixtures, recessed and ceiling spots, and over-size vase floor lamps, which illuminate as well as display sculptural fronds of tropical greens. In keeping with the camp-bed silhouette, bedcovers are luxurious gray blankets. Walls throughout the hotel are composed of bands of horizontal granite bricks. The solidity of the stone is counterbalanced with the transparence of glass panels and smoked mirrors. Floors are gray stone or ebony parquet enlivened with a scarlet or olive shag rug.

While striving for purity and simplicity, each design element has enough force of personality that Pillet has created an idiosyncratic Sezz look that conveys the personality and taste of the owner. Kalaidjian and his wife are ardent collectors and promoters of contemporary art. When he purchased the hotel, Shahé says it was a Best Western "which had been run with a lot of love and affection for forty years by a couple." The Kalaidjians commissioned American photographer Stacie McCormick, who lives and works in London, to create "a photographic memory of the old hotel." Her large, evocative photographs, many of which focus on a Proustian detail such as a door handle or mosaic floor, are hung in the central stairwell and several rooms. A second photo series, on urban reflections, by Claudia Sorbac, was shot in New York. The reflection theme has a strong corollary with the design of the hotel, where reflection plays an integral role. Charlotte Kalaidjian runs the arts organization Room for My Art, which exhibits in hotels the work of mostly young emerging artists.

A unique Sezz feature is La Grande Dame bar, named for the stout bottle synonymous with Veuve Clicquot Champagne's prestige cuvée produced from a blend of Chardonnay and Pinot Noir grapes. While other beverages are available, the only Champagne on offer is the one with the tangerine label. The sky-lit bar is furnished with a pair of circular booths upholstered in hot-pink leather, made to order for a romantic tête-à-tête. Additional services include the Well-Being area with Jacuzzi and steam and massage rooms, a ten-person meeting room, and twenty-four-hour room service.

It's no surprise that the tailored minimalist décor, personal assistants ready to streamline schedules, chic meeting room, and quiet bar have made Sezz popular with International businessmen. If James Bond were looking for an incognito Parisian retreat, you could safely recommend it.

SHAHÉ KALAIDJIAN'S COUPS DE COEUR

RESTAURANT
AKASAKA
9, rue Nicolo, 75016
Tel.: 01 42 88 77 86
Ranked among the top Japanese restaurants in the city. Very welcoming, with irreproachable quality and attractive Zen décor.

LANDMARK—ARCHITECTURE
CASTEL BÉRANGER
14, rue la Fontaine, 75016
Landmark art nouveau building that made the reputation of French architect Hector Guimard, who also designed the iconic wrought-iron and glass Métro exits, synonymous with this very Parisian style.

MONUMENT
LA TOUR EIFFEL
Place du Trocadéro, 75016
www.tour-eiffel.fr
Visible from two suites at Sezz but spectacular viewed across the Seine from the square between the Palais de Chaillot and Musée de l'Homme as it lights up after sunset.

MUSEUM
MAISON DE BALZAC
47, rue Raynouard, 75016
Tel.: 01 55 74 41 80
Balzac's sole remaining Parisian residence, where he edited his *Comédie Humaine* and wrote several classics. On display are personal effects, first editions, manuscripts, artwork, and memorabilia of his era.

GOURMET FOOD – COVERED MARKET
MARCHÉ DE PASSY
Corner of rue Duban and rue Bois-le-Vent, 75016
Metro: La Muette
Tuesday through Friday 8:00 A.M.-1:00 P.M. & 4:00 P.M.-7:00 P.M.
Saturday 8:00 A.M.-1:00 P.M. & 3:30 P.M.-7:00 P.M.
Sunday 8:00 A.M.-1:00 P.M.
Soup-to-nuts gourmet and fresh produce to meet demanding standard of neighborhood clientele. Stock up for impromptu vacation picnic and back home gift list.

LE PLACIDE

Luxe, calme, et lucidité

Jean Pierre Bansard
6, rue Saint-Placide
75006 Paris
www.leplacidehotel.com

MUCH AS PRECIOUS GIFTS tend to come in small packages, this intimate hotel designed on a human scale offers a concentration of subtle luxuries and quiet beauty. Bruno Borrione, who has collaborated for two decades with Philippe Starck, created a sensitive total design project. While less theatrical, Borrione's vision incorporates strains of his mentor's fire-and-ice aesthetic. Pure lines and minimal ornamentation are warmed by rosewood paneling, luminous green walls, a smattering of Missoni and Kenzo print cushions, and Cole & Son graphic winter-woods wallpaper.

Geometric furniture created for the hotel includes elegant built-in white leather banquettes and matching oversize headboards in the eleven junior suites. Variety is achieved through color variation. Each floor has its color scheme—almond green, ochre, black-and-white, taupe, or mauve. There are two suites per floor extending along the length of the building, with a bedroom window on the street side and a bathroom window opening onto a private inner courtyard (where you can't be seen). A glass wall separating bed and bathrooms that can be camouflaged by a curtain enhances the luxury of natural light at different moments of the day. Beveled mirrors strategically placed in guest rooms and ground-floor spaces add volume to a narrow structure.

Bathrooms are minimalist white. A sculptural tub beckons visitors to indulge in a peaceful soak before slipping into the cushy toweling robe and kabuki slippers. If there were a prize for best-designed and highest-quality amenities, Placide would be in the running. The bathroom scale, makeup mirror, hangers, translucent Post-It notes, and beribboned and bejeweled key ring are design standouts. An iPod base and gift bag with city guides and souvenir laundry bag in unbleached cotton are useful extras.

Attention to quality extends to the gourmet breakfast buffet with cheese from Barthélemy, the Left Bank's premier *fromagerie*, and organic fresh produce from La Grande Épicerie down the block at the Bon Marché department store.

The buffet set up in the front window has nothing to hide. Fresh fruit salad, lean charcuterie, fresh-baked whole-grain rolls, olives, a selection of dried fruits and nuts, muesli, and perfectly ripened cheese are confirmation that you are

OPPOSITE:
Colored cushions and bed throws inject a slash of color into a predominately white, minimalist palette.

OPPOSITE LEFT:
A sleek, built-in
banquette optimizes
space.

OPPOSITE TOP RIGHT:
Night table appointed
with chic clock radio and
translucent note pad.

OPPOSITE BOTTOM RIGHT:
A glass wall enhances
the flow of natural light
from the bedroom and
bathroom windows.

being taken care of by a sophisticated and discerning Parisian. Your hostess, Marie Garabedian, leaves nothing to chance. Flowers are one of her passions, and stylish arrangements are created by aptly named l'Artisan Fleuriste.

Garabedian attributes twenty years as an optician for "teaching me the importance of rigor, technique, and intransigence when it comes to detail." She also worked as an antiques dealer specializing in silver and enjoyed a close collaboration with Borrione on the hotel's creation. She lauds his talent as a colorist and a master of space, and his refusal to compromise on the minutiae of his concept. Hotel owner Jean Pierre Bansard, whose privately held Cible Corporation recently purchased Peugeot's Solex electric bike line, has provided guests with a pair of bikes. Bansard recently introduced another green feature—a biodegradable duvet cover for each guest, which is disposed of after they leave.

The scale and refinement of the Placide reflect a Japanese sensibility, and the hotel quickly became popular with this clientele, who also appreciate proximity to world-class shopping. Bon Marché, incontestably the most Parisian of department stores, is a minute away, and the highest concentration of designer shoe stores in the city is a five-minute walk toward Saint-Germain. Rue Saint-Placide is also a shopping destination with its cluster of designer discount outlets.

In addition to fashion and design temptations, the residential neighborhood is well serviced by bistros, *boulangeries*, and established boutiques catering to an exigent native clientele.

With just eleven rooms, the ambiance at Placide is relaxed and familial. The lounge is stocked with piles of magazines for perusing by the fireplace, and a drinks cart can be moved onto the terrace for an aperitif under the olive tree in fair weather. A full range of services is available to enhance your visit, including a personal shopper and trainer and beauty services from massage to pedicure. Garabedian compiles a bimonthly listing of events she feels will be of particular interest to guests, and the youthful, energetic staff is always responsive to special requests.

BOUTIQUE—CHILDREN'S CLOTHING,
BOOKS AND FURNISHINGS
BONTON BAZAR
122, rue du Bac, 75007
Tel.: 01 42 22 77 69
Monday–Saturday, 10 A.M.–7 P.M.
Concept store that sees the home though a child's eyes with an irre-sistible selection of furniture, clothing, books, and accessories.

ANTIQUES
FARMAN
122, rue du Bac, 75007
Tel.: 01 45 44 87 39
Antiques and bric-a-brac from airplane propellors to chandeliers.

RESTAURANT
LE GORILLE BLANC
11 bis, rue Chomel, 75007
Tel.: 01 45 49 04 54
Traditional neighborhood bistro with southwest-inspired menu, a
warm welcome, and irreproachable service.

BOUTIQUE—ARTISAN
MISIA RÊVE
87, rue du Bac, 75007
Tel.: 01 42 84 20 52
Monday–Saturday, 11 A.M.–7 P.M.
Claudine Couppé's hand-painted and serigraphic canvas and leather
accessories featuring the musings of her fictional character Misia Rêve
make trendy Parisian gifts.

FLORIST
L'ARTISAN FLEURISTE
6, rue de Commaille, 75007
Tel.: 01 42 84 40 41
Inventive contemporary arrangements. Staff is happy to collaborate
with clients in the creation of bouquets.

OPPOSITE LEFT:
Alaia boutique next door to
5, rue de Moussy.

OPPOSITE RIGHT:
Trompe l'oeil seriograph print and
Saarinen Tulip chair, Petit Moulin.

Couture

5, RUE DE MOUSSY
(4th), Hôtel-de-Ville
Modernist pied-à-terre

HOTEL DU PETIT MOULIN
(3rd), Marais
Made to measure by Lacroix

Two of France's most admired and iconoclastic couturiers are the creative spirits behind intimate hotels with contrasting personalities located in the historic Marais district. Christian Lacroix, who lives near the Petit Moulin, became involved in its creation through neighborly curiosity, while Azzedine Alaia is the proprietor of 5, rue de Moussy. Neither is a native of Paris, but both built their careers there and personify a standard of sophistication and culture that reinforces the city's reputation as the capital of fashion.

Much as Alaia's and Lacroix's clothing collections reflect a clearly defined aesthetic and vision of the feminine ideal, the hotel concepts are an extension of their personal design philosophies. Lacroix, synonymous with color and pattern, and historical and cultural references, produced a richly hued eclectic patchwork interior synthesizing myriad influences. Alaia, who wears a monastic uniform of black Mandarin-style jacket and cloth slippers, created a contemplative minimalist environment to house his collection of modernist furniture. These divergent perspectives symbolize the multifaceted character of the Marais district, which encompasses historic Île Saint-Louis and Place de Vosges as well as contemporary Les Halles and the Beaubourg museum.

5, RUE DE MOUSSY

Modernist pied-à-terre

Azzedine Alaia
5, rue de Moussy
75004 Paris
www.3rooms-5ruedemoussy.com

ZZEDINE ALAIA IS KNOWN FOR shunning theatrics and letting his exquisitely crafted clothes do the talking. The same can be said for the décor of the sleekly urbane guest house he created for friends and friends of friends. The three lower floors of the five-story eighteenth-century building in the Marais have been transformed into one- and two-bedroom apartments equipped for long- or short-term stays. An austere steel front door punched with a geometric design foreshadows the contemporary transformation within. The original central staircase was preserved, but there is now an elevator to deliver guests to their private floor, where they can settle into a pied-à-terre with the bonus of room-service breakfast.

If Alaia is somewhat reclusive, he can be quite sociable with his creative team and coterie of good friends. When he acquired the building adjacent to a complex housing his boutique, atelier, and workrooms, the concept of converting it into a guest house had greater appeal than developing a block of flats with long-term leases.

Architect Bernard Bouchet has created minimalist interiors to complement the couturier's extensive collection of contemporary designer furniture, including many rare original pieces. The bold sculptural aesthetic of furniture and light fixtures by Jean Prouvé, Marc Newson, Serge Mouille, Jean Nouvel, and Arne Jacobsen correlates perfectly with the sexy curves and razor-fine tailoring of Alaia couture. As with his clothing collections, solid colors prevail over pattern; flashes of red, cobalt, or yellow accentuate black, white, and neutral shades. When it came to equipping the apartments, no detail escaped the perfectionist who can cut and sew a garment with the same dexterity and attention to minutiae as the legendary *petites mains* in his workrooms. The selection of artwork is limited to paintings of subtle beauty by Christophe von Weyhe from a series entitled *Port of Hamburg by Night*. Kitchens have everything necessary for fixing a snack or laying the table for an impromptu take-out dinner. Well-equipped office set-ups encourage productive working visits. Unexpected amenities include below-floor radiant heating, white Havana thongs in place of terry slippers, and a selection of fine teas.

There is a monastic beauty to the polished cement floors and simple opaque shades filtering sunlight from the row of windows overlooking the rue de Moussy.

OPPOSITE:
Original Jean Prouvé
Compas dining table,
Standard chairs and
Bahut cabinet.

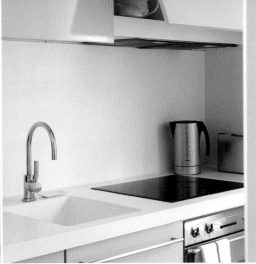

ABOVE FROM LEFT:
Illuminated Metro sign,
Hotel de Ville.

One of the well-equipped
kitchens.

Sculptural molded wood
stool, bathroom.

OPPOSITE LEFT:
Dramatic Serge Mouille
sconce with four rotating
arms, bedroom.

OPPOSITE RIGHT:
Kwo Hoi Chan Lemon Sole
chair and painting by
Christophe Von Weyhe

OVERLEAF
LEFT:
Pair of Pierre
Paulin couches.

RIGHT:
White marble interior,
Alaia shoe boutique.

Despite being a stone's throw from the Hôtel de Ville and the BHV department store, the narrow one-way street feels like a secluded location. It's a lively neighborhood filled with boutiques and galleries. Excursion options radiate in every direction, and place des Vosges, the Seine, Île de Saint Louis, Nôtre Dame, the Beaubourg and Picasso museums, and the historic Marais neighborhood are readily accessible on foot.

Guest-house manager Patrice Brunel greets you on arrival to hand over keys and make sure you are comfortably settled. His warm, friendly manner and knowledge of the neighborhood make him a valued resource throughout your stay. Guests have as much autonomy as they wish, since a room-service breakfast is optional. The layout of the three apartments is well suited for couples traveling as a group or families with older children. While the chic austerity of the setting isn't designed for families with toddlers, the one-bedroom apartment is a serene retreat for parents seeking a break from them. To maintain selectivity, 5, rue de Moussy relies on word of mouth rather than active promotion.

The clothing and shoe boutiques in the adjoining building are not to be missed, providing as they do a discreet glimpse into the world of an internationally respected couturier. Don't be intimidated by the buzzer, and be sure to glance into the central fitting room, where a broken-plate portrait of Alaia by good friend Julian Schnabel is propped up against a wall. The boutique's interior, designed by Schnabel, is more SoHo loft than Saint-Honoré formal. However, a new white marble shoe boutique is a minimalist temple displaying some of the sexiest footwear around. Shoe fetishists be on guard.

AZZEDINE ALAIA'S COUPS DE COEUR

GOURMET FOOD—BUTCHER
BOUCHERIE GARDIL
44, rue Saint-Louis-en-l'Île, 75004
Tel.: 01 43 54 97 15
Closed Sunday morning and Monday.
In matters of taste, quality ingredients rate as highly with Alaia as fine fabric. To ensure that his employees eat well, he has a chef in residence that cooks lunch every day for the entire staff. This award-winning butcher meets his meticulous standards.

GOURMET FOOD—ICE CREAM
MAISON BERTHILLON
29–31, rue Saint-Louis-en-l'Île, 75004
Tel.: 01 43 54 31 61 | www.berthillon.fr
Founded on the Île Saint Louis in 1954, a fourth generation of Berthillons upholds the family motto, "Quality is Our Passion." Only natural ingredients go into forty flavors of ice cream and sorbet.

DEPARTMENT STORE—HARDWARE
BHV RIVOLI—SOUS-SOL
14, rue du Temple, 75004
Tel.: 01 42 74 90 00 | www.bhv.fr
Monday–Saturday, 9:30 A.M.–7:30 P.M.; Wednesday until 9 P.M.
The largest and best stocked hardware store in the city is located in a sprawling basement next door to City Hall around the corner from 5, rue de Moussy. It recently underwent a redesign but retains its quirky charm despite the streamlining.

MUSEUM
MUSÉE PICASSO
Hôtel Salé
5, rue de Thorigny, 75003
Tel.: 01 42 71 25 21 | www.musee-picasso.fr
Tax-saving bequests to the state by Picasso's children and widow Jacqueline form the basis of this extensive collection housed in a magnificent seventeenth-century mansion. Diego Giacometti, favored model of his brother the painter and sculptor, designed the fixtures and furnishings.

RESTAURANT
L'OSTERIA
10, rue Sévigné, 75004
Tel.: 01 42 71 37 08
Closed all day Saturday, Sunday, and Monday noon.
Patronized by a chic international clientele, this unmarked trattoria with the allure of a private club is welcoming to the uninitiated. The gnocchi and risotto are luscious. Good selection of Italian wines.

HÔTEL DU PETIT MOULIN

Made to measure by Lacroix

Nadia Murano
29/31, rue de Poitou
75003 Paris
www.hoteldupetitmoulin.com

F YOU PULLED UP IN A TAXI at Hôtel du Petit Moulin without knowing its secret, you'd swear the driver had the wrong address. Perched on a timeless corner of the Haut-Marais, it passes at first glance for a picturesque boulangerie—which it was for three hundred years. When the last baguette was sold in 2000, "the little mill" was reputed to be the city's oldest bakery, with a legacy of illustrious clients, including Victor Hugo. Notable current neighbor, the couturier Christian Lacroix, values the Marais's village ambiance and kept a watchful eye on the transformation of the historic landmark and adjoining seventeenth-century building, which housed an old bar and residential hotel. When Lacroix learned it was a hotel project, he arranged to meet the owners and persuaded them he was the ideal candidate to design the interior.

The happy result is a Pandora's box of ambiances reflecting the many facets of the Marais past and present channeled via the exuberant aesthetic of a designer acclaimed for his genius as a colorist and knack for appropriating and synthesizing French history and regional culture. The hotel's patchwork of interiors aptly reflects the spirit of its surroundings: narrow streets that escaped the template of urban planner Baron Haussmann's realignment of the city in the 1860s and which are now animated by a hive of innovative boutiques, galleries, and eateries. As at the Petit Moulin, local merchants keep signage to a minimum, which lends to shopping the pleasure of discovery.

Lacroix likens his approach to interior design to the philosophy underpinning his collections: "It's like couture, where the harmony is created from a jigsaw of influences, where the mood of the moment is nourished by elements of the past, where modernity lives in the tradition of the present." He relished the challenge of working with a new set of volumes and parameters, admitting that designing a hotel fulfilled a lingering desire: "I had the impression of rediscovering a childhood dream left along the wayside."

The discreet visionary behind the project as a whole is slender, sleekly elegant Nadia Murano, who purchased the property with her husband, Denis Nourry, in 2003 after a failed quest for an existing hotel in need of transformation. Petit Moulin is her baptism in the hotel business and she appreciated the serendipity of collaboration between two outsiders fulfilling a mutual dream. She has a point

OPPOSITE:
Lobby lounge with Arco floor lamp and colorful ceramic India Mahdavi Bishop stools.

OPPOSITE TOP, FROM LEFT:
The elevator is papered in a Lacroix-designed seriograph.

Bathroom mirror replicates signature Lacroix heart motif.

A convex mirror is one of the many playful visual illusions used by Lacroix.

The color scheme of Room 204 is slate blue accented with ruby red.

OPPOSITE BOTTOM:
Dreamy cosmic collage in Room 302, overlooking rue de Poitou.

of view and did not hesitate to express it during the project, but gave Lacroix free rein within the confines of a budget.

The ornate painted glass facade and interior of the bakeshop—both listed on the historic register—were incorporated into the new design. Restored wall panels and a ceiling adorned with pastoral scenes, original mirrors, and almond-green woodwork enhanced by ruffled aubergine taffeta shades and a Venetian glass chandelier give the lobby a sugar-icing ambiance. The mood shifts from the confectionary lobby to a soigné lounge furnished with black leather and chrome couches, a 1960s Arco floor lamp, and quartet of sculptural India Mahdavi ceramic Bishop stools.

The character of each room is a response to its proportions, ceiling height, and view. Floor plans reflect the organic contours of the historic structure, reinforcing the sense of a house where everyone has a customized retreat. While the seventeen rooms have individualized décor, key themes persist—the playful juxtaposition of historic vernacular and architectural detail with modernist furnishings and materials. Lacroix makes clever use of trompe-l'oeil collages and mirrors throughout. The wall behind a bed might feature a reworked blowup of a page from the designer's sketchbook or a fanciful celestial collage. But as with the refined interplay of texture, print, and color in Lacroix's couture collections, he achieves improbably harmonious balance with unexpected interior combinations. Graphic patterns and vibrant colors are tempered by polished cement floors, exposed wood beams, or sober felted draperies, so that no element overwhelms the whole. Masculine segues to femininity, rococo folly to minimalist restraint. Bathrooms serve as another counterpoint to each room's mood. A baroque suite features a minimalist slate tiled bath, while a neo-pop bedroom is paired with a nostalgic bathroom complete with claw-foot tub and chain-pull toilet.

The massive seventeenth-century wood staircase connecting the floors of the former inn have been stripped of old paint and the steps carpeted in graphic black and white polka dots. On landings, stairwell walls have been replaced with glass for added light and visual intrigue.

As is the trend in many boutique hotels, the bistro-style bar does double duty as breakfast room, when the Belle-Époque–style tables are dressed in white linen. The retro zinc bar pays homage to the former establishment even if today the clientele is restricted to guests and their friends. Settling into a cushioned banquette, illuminated by hanging lamps with softly shifting colored lights, puts you in an escapist mood; it's a time-travel fantasy skillfully transmitted to guests in this made-to-measure hideaway.

OPPOSITE:
Lacroix created a fashion fantasia mural rich in historic reference for room 302.

RIGHT:
Hanging lamps shift from pink to green and blue in the colorfully appointed bar.

RESTAURANT
CHEZ NÉNESSE

17, rue de Saintonge, 75003
Tel.: 01 42 78 46 49
Closed weekends and holidays.
This family-run bistro directly opposite the hotel, with a stove heater
in the middle of the dining room and red-check tablecloths, retains the
soul of a working-class canteen. Madame Lelu is behind the bar and
Monsieur in the kitchen. Portions are as hearty as the welcome.

BOUTIQUE—INTERIOR DESIGN
THE COLLECTION

33, rue de Poitou, 75003
Tel.: 01 42 77 04 20 | www.thecollection.fr | thecollection@wanadoo.fr
British-born Alison Grant caught the attention of the shelter press
with her series of wallpapers by French, British, and Danish artists
that are a crossover between craft and design. Forty percent of her
stock is British made, but she promotes emerging French and Scandi-
navian artists and designers. Christian Lacroix selected a number of
her serigraphic trompe-l'oeil papers and silhouette decal stickers for
the décor of the hotel.

CAFÉ BAR
LE PROGRÉS

1, rue de Bretagne, 75003
Tel.: 01 42 72 01 44
Another Lacroix pick. Popular neighborhood gathering place dominat-
ing the corner of rue Vieille du Temple. Great Parisian vibe and well
positioned for people watching.

MARKET—GOURMET FOOD AND RESTAURANTS
LE MARCHÉ DES ENFANTS-ROUGES

39, rue de Bretagne, 75003
Tuesday–Sunday.
The city's oldest market, named for orphans dressed in red who occupied an orphanage on the site until 1777, when it became a covered
market. The twenty or so stalls propose a mix of French fare and exotic
takeout. As popular for the eateries as for running errands.

BOUTIQUES
LE MARAIS

Nadia encourages guests to explore neighborhood boutiques. There is a
high concentration of young designers, galleries, and design and accessories shops stocked with original gifts and one-of-a-kind creations.

OPPOSITE, CLOCKWISE FROM TOP LEFT:
Hot-pink oversize arabesque
wallpaper, Général.

Detail, lounge table and
armchairs, Banville.

Line up of sculptural
armchairs, de Sers.

Lucite bubble chairs, bar
mezzanine, Kube.

Bar lounge

GÉNÉRAL
(11th), *Oberkampf*
High design with a smile

HOTEL DE BANVILLE
(17th), *Rue de Courcelles*
Art deco update

KUBE
(18th), *Montmartre*
Where it's kool to be square

DE SERS
(8th), *Georges V*
Simply impeccable

Not by chance, three of the four Bar Lounge hotel selections are located off the beaten track of tourism. Young-at-heart Général and Kube are in hip neighborhoods experiencing gentrification, with vibrant music and club scenes, respectively, around the Marais and Obérkampf or Pigalle and Montmartre.

The others are in bourgeois arrondissements—the Banville in a residential section of the 17th and De Sers, the most elegant and luxurious of the quartet, on the border of the 8th and 16th off exclusive avenue Georges V. All four have contemporary décor, although Kube is indisputably the coolest in terms of innovative design features.

Hotel bars with live music are a rarity, but the Banville has the distinction of being owned by an elegant cabaret singer who performs on Tuesday night. Kube has an eclectic music scene featuring international DJs. On "Girly Wednesday," women spin the mixes and live performers from jazz singers to acoustic guitarists are regularly scheduled.

GÉNÉRAL

High design with a smile

Gilles Douillard
5/7, rue Rampon
75011 Paris
Legeneralhotel.com

𝒯HE GÉNÉRAL APPEALS to the irrepressible kid within, the part that enjoys freebies, comic strips, and Kinder eggs. There must be plenty of us out there, as the hotel director Franck Altruie claims that his bar clientele scoop up kilos per week of rainbow-hued Haribo candies set out in dishes. Candy is the first of many treats on offer. A silvery rubber duck is ready to share your bath, and a bright-green apple is nestled in the dimple atop your crisp white bed pillow, while a range of Occidental bath products are set to pamper and a snack tray with biscuits and Kusmi tea is provided for a peckish moment. The Général is one of few Parisian hotels where a teakettle is standard equipment in guest rooms.

An array of six supplements from omega-3 to anti-age and bronzing boosters are set out with the breakfast buffet, and room service offers Lebanese, Japanese, and Indian menus along with a classic French option. Even the ground-floor raspberry and chocolate color scheme evokes pleasant connotations, and exuberant arrangements of bright tropical orchids are the happiest flowers in town. The youthful staff has an upbeat energy to match the cool soundtrack and zesty colors surrounding them.

Gilles Douillard, founder of the DeVille and Le Quartier boutique hotel groups, set himself a challenge to provide great design and service in neighborhoods undergoing rapid gentrification on the east side of Paris for significantly less than comparable hotels in the central and affluent western arrondissements. A demand exists, and his group has added boutique hotels in both the Bastille and Bercy neighborhoods, although the Général, situated south of République between the Marais and trendy rue Oberkampf, was his first and remains the best appointed.

Top interior designer Jean-Philippe Nuel took a contemporary tack but plays with classical elements like the fuchsia and white arabesque motif blown up and painted onto fabric on walls in the lobby and bar. In the bar, which doubles as breakfast room, neo-pop white and chrome chairs and tables are interspersed with club chairs upholstered in nubby Chanelesque knits. The pink theme is reprised in lounge areas on either side of the entrance. A giant peony print and jumbo translucent white floor lamp continue the oversize motif.

OPPOSITE:
Top-floor suite with signature granny smith apples posed on bed pillows.

ABOVE, FROM LEFT:
Attention to detail.

Vibrant shag pillow is
a cheeky accent on a
tailored grey sofa.

A silver rubber duck
is one of many fun
hospitality extras.

OPPOSITE TOP:
The forties facade was
treated to a whitewash
face-lift.

OPPOSITE BOTTOM,
FROM LEFT:
Detail, top-floor suite.

Art deco wrought-iron
balustrade

Double sinks are a stan-
dard feature in suites.

Hallways are carpeted in
a zippy pink-and-purple
checkerboard pattern.

The 1940s brick building was transformed into a gleaming whitewashed edifice with the blessing of the 11th arrondissement's mayor. Forties design elements like rosette balcony motifs add Parisian flair to views from rooms along the front of the hotel, which are nicely angled to catch the light and overlook the flower-filled balconies of a residential building opposite.

Room décor in shades of anthracite, camel, and café au lait is more subdued, with an occasional shot of color from a hot-pink-and-white zebra-patterned armchair or shaggy magenta ribbon pillow on a slate-gray couch. Furniture is geometric in smooth natural and dark wood with brushed chrome hardware. Junior suites and a more spacious suite under the eaves are excellent deals. A galley passage with designer double sinks divides the sitting room and bedrooms of the junior suites, and a bathtub/shower is recessed into the wall at the foot of the bed. Guest room artwork is black-and-white photography of Paris at its most glamorous and mysterious.

The neighborhood has several popular concert venues including the venerable Bataclan, and the hotel brochure notes that the Général is ready to receive guests around the clock. The hip hotel bar, open until 2 a.m. with a good play list and smiling bartender, has garnered favorable Parisian press and draws a neighborhood clientele. It is equally a hit with the thirty-five to fifty-five set who comprise the bulk of the guest register. A healthy alternative is the well-equipped fitness center and sauna, where you can begin or end the day with a workout in another cheerful setting.

FRANCK ALTRUIE'S COUPS DE COEUR

RESTAURANT
ASTIER

44, rue Jean-Pierre Timbaud, 75011
Tel.: 01 43 57 16 35 | www.restaurant-astier.com
Open daily.
A modest menu featuring traditional bistro fare. The main attraction here is a well-stocked wine cellar. A neighborhood institution beloved for its authenticity and lack of pretension.

RESTAURANT
LE PAMPHLET

38, rue Debelleyme, 75003
Tel.: 01 42 72 39 24
Closed Saturday and Monday lunch and Sunday.
Chef Alain Carrère, who trained at the Hôtel Crillon, proposes a weekly market menu in addition to house specials. Modern take on regional cuisine from the southwest complemented by *vins du terroir*.

BAR—AFTER HOURS
CAFÉ CHARBON

109, rue Oberkampf, 75011
Tel.: 01 43 57 57 40
On a street renowned for low-key *tendence* café-bars, Charbon is one of the trendiest. Action warms up after hours in the upper-floor dance hall. Sidewalk terrace, brasserie menu, and weekend brunch.

BOUTIQUE—FASHION/DESIGN
LIEU COMMUN (MATALI CRASSET AND RON ORB)

5, rue des Filles du Calvaire, 75003
Tel.: 01 44 54 08 30 | www.lieucommun.fr
Tuesday–Saturday.
Design cooperative that captures the spirit of the neighborhood. Crasset's futuristic organic decorative objects animate hip urban sportswear. A micro music label adds a third dimension to the concept.

BAR/BISTRO
CLOWN BAR

114, rue Amelot, 75011
Tel.: 01 43 55 87 35 | www.clown-bar.fr
Open daily.
Two doors up from Cirque d'Hiver, the colorful venue built in 1852 for cold-weather circus performances, this atmospheric retro bistro with a charming circus-themed décor has hosted international circus acts for a century. Pre-fixe menus offered at lunch and dinner.

OPPOSITE:
The overscale floor lamp
is a glowing focal point
of the lobby salon.

RIGHT:
Bowls of rainbow
Haribo candy make a
playful bar snack.

HÔTEL DE BANVILLE

Art deco update

Marianne Moreau
166, boulevard Berthier
75017 Paris
www.hotelbanville.fr

UPON ENTERING THE BANVILLE, the first thing that catches your attention is a glossy black grand piano on an elegant circular rug rimmed with twinkling fiber-optic lights—displayed like a sexy sports car in a showroom. This surprising lobby fixture actually fits in perfectly with the hotel's neo–art deco ambiance and is more than a decorative prop: owner Marianne Moreau moonlights as a singer Tuesday evenings, when lights dim and the chic ground-floor lounge transforms into a cabaret bar. Moreau has no qualms indulging her love of performing, having spent a lifetime in and around the hotel, opened by her grandmother and mother the year she was born. A vivacious blonde with the effortless chic and inbred confidence of a seasoned Parisian hostess, Moreau clearly enjoys people and is delighted to entertain guests. She encourages other musicians to drop in Tuesday nights.

The glamorous bar with minimalist freestanding fireplace is one of several features Moreau introduced since taking the helm ten years ago. With the collaboration of her architect husband, she refurbished the 1926 building to reposition it as an intimate four-star establishment in the spirit of the bourgeois 17th arrondissement neighborhood in which it is situated. While the ambiance of ground-floor reception areas, the staircase, and hallways exudes streamlined sophistication, guest room décor is more eclectic and romantic. Having witnessed the Banville thrive under the direction of three generations of women, Moreau respects the importance of feminine influence.

Throughout the hotel, warm red is the signature counterpoint to a sleek architectural framework of creamy marble floors and limestone walls highlighted with deco wrought-iron balustrades, blond wood, and burnished hammered steel. Particular attention has been paid to elegant lighting design and comfortable upholstered seating, creating a soothing environment that encourages guests to settle in and relax at any moment of the day.

Tablecloths transform the piano into a clever breakfast buffet, and guests tend to linger in the lounge's bright daytime mood. In a nod to the establishment's heritage, Moreau has hung a group of nineteenth- and early-twentieth-century portraits, landscapes, and still-life paintings inherited from her grandmother

OPPOSITE:
A gleaming grand piano
is the star of the lobby.

OPPOSITE LEFT:
Tables set for breakfast in the salon.

OPPOSITE TOP RIGHT:
Glossy red guest-room doors resemble the entry to a townhouse.

OPPOSITE BOTTOM RIGHT:
Original art deco architectural detail of entryway viewed from salon.

around the ground floor, which adds a retro, domestic touch. Cozy seating on either side of the open fireplace is just right for perusing the selection of newspapers and magazines while enjoying a cocktail.

Along upstairs corridors, frosted glass strips etched with room names inset at the threshold of guest rooms dramatically light up glossy red doors with brass knobs resembling a row of townhouses. The rooms are named after family members or the theme of the décor, and each has a personalized style.

Most rooms overlook the avenue and enjoy ample daylight. The top-floor suite benefits from the additional perk of a rooftop view of the Eiffel Tower. Predominant color schemes are white, taupe, or beige contrasted with accents of red, black, brown, or mauve. The mood ranges from classic to contemporary, with upholstered furnishings and decorative light fixtures softening the graphic effect. Red woodwork and check fabric in the Pastoral rooms evoke a chalet mood, while the Prelude rooms have handsome headboards upholstered in red alligator leather. Bathrooms are integrated into rooms in theatrical alcoves hung with sweeping drapes, which can be drawn for privacy. All are attractively appointed with retro clawfoot tubs or contemporary black marble sinks depending on the theme of the room.

Clever lighting isn't limited to interior effects. At night the geometric elegance of the building's 1920s facade is given a glamorous makeover with subtle lights illuminating sculptural detail in rosy sunrise and sunset hues. Moreau got tired of people saying they hadn't noticed there was a hotel in the neighborhood and is amused that the installation established the Banville as a distinctive landmark without resorting to commercial signage. Like it's stylish owner, the Banville turns heads with the allure of cool sophistication.

HÔTEL
DE
BANVILLE

★★★

RESTAURANT—BISTRO

PHÉBÉ

190, rue de Courcelles, 75017

Tel.: 01 46 22 33 23

The 1905 art nouveau décor of this charming bistro dates from its start as a shop selling rum imported from Martinique. Poppies, hollyhocks, and other kitchen-garden flowers adorn the tiled walls. Owner Alain Liègre tends bar and chats with regulars, who refer to it as their canteen. Traditional menu with daily specials.

GOURMET–BAKERY

R. MAEDER–BOULANGERIE PATISSERIE ALSACIENNE

158, boulevard Berthier, 75017

Tel.: 01 46 22 50 73 | boulangerie-alsace.com

The baguettes here are so good that President Jacques Chirac is rumored to have had them delivered to the Élysée Palace. The almond-paste–filled *galette des rois* (Epiphany cake) was a 2004 Best of Paris laureate.

SHOPPING

RUE DE COURCELLES, 75017

Quintessential bourgeois high street for everything from housewares, children's wear, and fashion accessories to cheese and *saucisson*.

PARK

PARC MONCEAU, 75017

An oasis of calm dotted with architectural follies, flowerbeds, and statues. Beautifully landscaped in an informal English style. Claude Monet painted five canvases here between 1876 and 1878.

RESTAURANT

BALTHAZAR

73, avenue Niel, 75017

Tel.: 01 44 40 28 15

Trendy neighborhood restaurant with a sophisticated contemporary ambiance serving updated French cuisine by Chef Benoit Vanheesbeke.

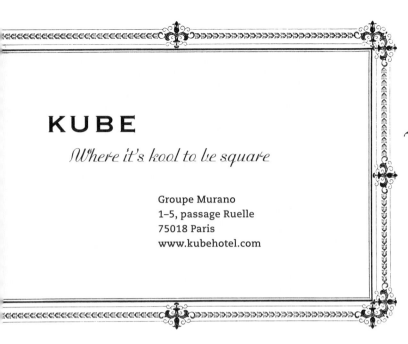

KUBE

Where it's kool to be square

Groupe Murano
1–5, passage Ruelle
75018 Paris
www.kubehotel.com

A CUL DE SAC on the border of Little India above Gare du Nord might stretch the hideaway concept for conventional souls but not *branché* Parisians who relish the novelty of staying at Kube Rooms and Bars for an escapist overnight adventure. Design hotels in improbable neighborhoods are nothing new to London, Madrid, or Rotterdam, but, pre-Kube, Parisian luxury hotels played it safe.

Proximity to the Eurostar high-speed train terminal tempers Kube's unconventional location for international guests who come to sip Grey Goose cocktails in the sub-zero Ice Kube Bar, sample chef Nicolas Guillard's inventive finger food, and chill out on Sundays over "Arty" brunch hosted by *Technikart* culture magazine, when an artist whose work is showcased is on hand for commentary and conversation.

Kube opted to position itself as emblematic of an attitude rather than mimic the hip hotel designer showcase formula. Extraordinary décor has driven the hotel's success, but it is the expression of a concept rather than the opus of a famous designer. Kube attitude is synonymous with innovation and the unexpected. The tone is set from the moment of arrival at an unmarked entry, which leads into the paved courtyard of a freshly renovated nineteenth-century building with a steep slate mansard roof. The reception area is housed in a minimalist glass and steel cube in the midst of the courtyard— an architectural juxtaposition echoing I. M. Pei's Louvre pyramid.

Behind Kube's listed historic facade, the interior is thoroughly contemporary. The heart of the building is dedicated to a vast lounge space with a two-story central well rimmed by a mezzanine housing the reservation-only Ice Kube Bar, a row of sculptural Lucite "bubble chairs" suspended from chains, and a DJ station. Facing the hotel entry is a sleek ten-meter bar, overhung with a fringe of fiber-optic lights, where elegant black-clad personnel are at the ready from mid-morning until the night's closing sound mix.

Innovation is integral to the Kube experience. In addition to the city's first ice bar, where the temperature hovers at 10 degrees Fahrenheit, it has two state-of-the-art screening rooms, digital-imprint door locks, and multifunction guest-room computers that double as TV and DVD player. Machines in the gym are

OPPOSITE:
The glass and steel reception area in the hotel's enclosed courtyard.

108

The sub-zero Ice Cube Bar.

equipped with individual entertainment screens, and the Nordic Room features a suspended bed and overflow tub illuminated by remote-controlled LED lights.

In guest rooms, a glacial theme is evoked by cube-shaped furniture in glass, resin, and Lucite, simulating ice. White predominates with accents of silver and fluorescent and powder pink. Faux-fur curtains and black-and-white photos of 1960s celebrities swathed in fashionable pelts warm up the mood. Lighting in hallways is deliberately obscure, but once you swipe a finger to open your room, the landing is flooded with daylight. The dazzling loft-design guest rooms ring the open courtyard and average two or more windows. An open-plan layout maximizes space. The bedroom might be separated from the bath by a glass brick wall that doubles as headboard. Flooring is silver-gray woven plastic, and curtains alternate between metallic netting and plush white faux fur. A hot-pink "baboom" animal pillow and pop-bead jeweled hangers provide decorative touches. The suspension theme is reprised as a clothing rail in lieu of a closet, the presumption being that one's wardrobe is so fabulous it merits the exposure.

The Ice Kube Bar is open Wednesday through Sunday from 7 p.m. to 2 a.m. Before entering, guests bundle up in hooded tundra parkas provided by Puma and polar fleece gloves. Sandals are ill advised. Bartenders whose shift lasts several hours look prepared to hit the slopes in Courchevel. The long narrow room that can accommodate a party of thirty is furnished with ice sculptures. The current décor includes an igloo, throne, and "chimney" mantles for posing drinks. When daylight filters through the glass block walls it is surprisingly bright, and by night it is bathed in waves of colored light. House recipe Grey Goose Vodka cocktails are served in conical ice goblets (hence the need for gloves). The whole experience is rather bracing and lots of fun for your designated half-hour visit.

By day, the lounge serves as a restaurant frequented primarily by hotel guests and business groups. Because the street is quiet, it is surprisingly tranquil and a great place to schedule a meeting or drink with friends. In fine weather, tables are set up in the courtyard, where the soundtrack is apt to be the timeless sounds of children playing during recess at the primary school next door—a reminder that some things never change.

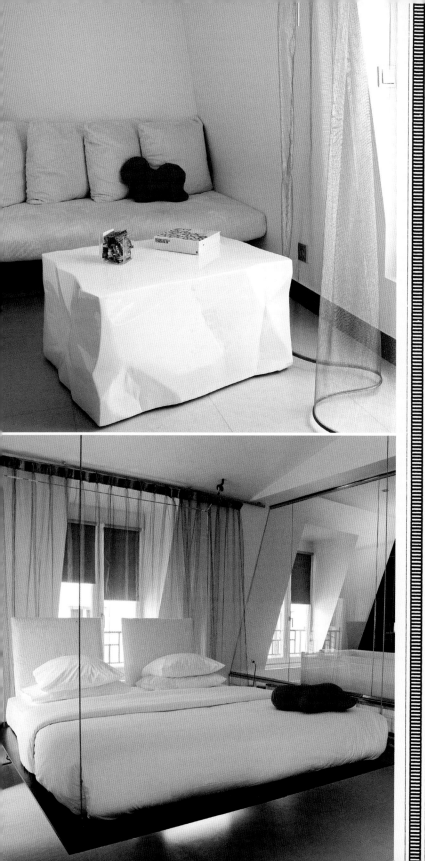

LAURENT VILAINE'S COUPS DE COEUR

LANDMARK
CANAL SAINT MARTIN

From square Frederick Lemaître to rue Lafayette, 75010
The 2001 film *Amélie Poulain* is credited with giving the canal international exposure, but Parisians had rediscovered its banks in the mid-1980s. An incursion of *bobo* (*bourgeois bohème*) restaurants, wine bars, and boutiques have made it an evening and weekend destination—especially in fair weather.

THEATER
LA REINE BLANCHE

2 bis, passage Ruelle, 75018
Tel.: 01 42 05 47 31 | www.reineblanche.com | reineblanche@free.fr
Opposite Kube is a young theater with an original program of music, theater, dance, and comedy, with performances Thursday through Sunday.

RESTAURANT
LE MOULIN DE LA GALETTE

83, rue Lepic, 75018
Tel.: 01 46 06 84 77 | www.lemoulindelagalette.fr
Open daily.
The recently renovated restaurant sits beneath a windmill dating from 1717 on the former site of a music hall immortalized by Renoir in *Bal du Moulin de la Galette* (Musée d'Orsay). Depending on the season, the warm contemporary interior space or two terraces promise a memorable meal in the heart of historic Montmartre.

RESTAURANT
LUI . . . L'INSOLENT

15, rue Caulaincourt, 75018
Tel.: 01 53 28 28 31
This petite restaurant is acclaimed by locals for its hospitality, attractive décor, and *surtout*—quality cuisine that should not stretch your budget.

RESTAURANT
LE COTTAGE MARCADET

151 bis, rue Marcadet, 75018
Tel.: 01 42 57 71 22 | www.cottagemarcadet.com
contact@cottagemarcadet.com
Gastronomy and Montmartre are hardly synonymous, but young chef Cyril Choisne chose less charted territory for his first restaurant after training in some of the city's top Michelin-star kitchens—including l'Apicius and le Grand Vefour. An edited menu permits him to eschew convention in the pursuit of subtle complexity.

OPPOSITE:
Roof terrace adjoining
the Nordic suite.

RIGHT:
A ten-meter bar, lit by
a fringe of fiber-optic
lights, spans the rear
wall of the main lounge.

DE SERS

Simply impeccable

Thibault Vidalenc
41, avenue Pierre 1er de Serbie
75008 Paris
www.hoteldesers.com

*I*N 1880 THE MARQUIS DE SERS was proprietor of this fashionable address between avenues Marceau and Georges V, where the 8th and 16th arrondissements meet. Though he might be surprised by recent modifications, he would have to concede that the current owner is keeping his old home up rather well. Thibault Vidalenc, who inherited the establishment (formerly called the Queen Elizabeth) from his grandmother, is an avowed perfectionist. His love of beauty and uncompromising nature serve him well as owner and president of a small luxury hotel striving to set a high standard for the new millennium. During eight years learning the family business, moving his way up to the post of manager, Vidalenc was formulating a renewal plan. In 2001 he traveled the world with his cousin, an architect, stopping at top hotels from London to Los Angeles and Hong Kong. They agreed it was important to break out of the Parisian mindset and tap into the international scene. Upon their return, Vidalenc closed the family hotel for refurbishment, and the pair went to work.

The new de Sers caused a bit of a stir when it opened in 2004. Those anticipating a hip minimalist hotel or another variation on the bordello-chic aesthetic inspired by Hotel Costes were intrigued by an original, very personal vision. Vidalenc describes the ambiance as "an evolution of an *hôtel particulier* as though it had stayed in the same family over time." Resolutely contemporary yet filled with respect for the past, it remains a work in progress as Vidalenc tweaks the formula in response to feedback from guests. He discovered that live piano music in the hotel bar, though very appealing to Americans, was not the kind of entertainment Europeans and locals sought to unwind. Live music has been replaced with contemporary mixes that are energizing without being invasive. Nothing is left to chance with an impeccable, hands-on owner who characterizes his involvement as "two hundred percent."

Vidalenc scoured Drouot auctions to assemble a very fine collection of nineteenth- century portraits that have been meticulously restored and framed. They are hung throughout the ground floor to great effect against limestone walls classically embellished with fluted pilasters, baseboard moldings, and inset panels. "I always lived in beautiful places" is how Vidalenc accounts for his highly trained eye.

OPPOSITE:
Eiffel tower view,
Panoramic suite
terrace.

OPPOSITE TOP:
Suite furnishings
include classic and
contemporary elements.
Armchairs upholstered
in Missoni print.

OPPOSITE BOTTOM LEFT:
Delivery of signature hot-
pink, long-stem roses.

OPPOSITE BOTTOM RIGHT:
Bathroom with balcony
view has both a claw-foot
tub and spacious shower.

A formal stairwell, which once swept up to first-floor drawing rooms, has been restored and now leads to salons reserved for special events. The creamy walls of the long entry gallery (which was formerly an open-air passage leading to the stables) are juxtaposed with violet carpeting. Sculptural wing chairs upholstered in warm gray form a dramatic chorus line along the length of the picture gallery. Grouped in pairs around low marble drinks tables, it is hard to pass by without being tempted to settle into one.

The restaurant and bar are prime features and have developed a steady neighborhood business clientele. The dining room and lounge bar overlook a garden terrace that serves as an outdoor dining room. Light, imaginative cuisine is beautifully presented, and the breakfast menu provides three options including "healthy start" and a more copious "American" breakfast, which passes for a late-start brunch. Smooth, lustrous wood walls, a Carrara marble bar, white leather and chrome armchairs, and marble-topped tables create a contemporary feel. The transitional library salon is in the same register of warm-gray felted upholstery and violet carpet as the entry gallery, with the graphic counterpoint of colorful neo-pop Missoni print cushions and upholstered side chairs. Flowers are a key element of the décor. Hot-pink roses and fuchsia African daisies are signature blooms. Indirect overhead lighting and minimalist floor lamps radiate a subtle glow.

The principal design elements of the ground floor are reprised in the guest rooms, with the addition of contemporary photography of nocturnal Parisian views. Pristine all-white marble bathrooms with a mirrored wall behind the sink epitomize Vidalenc's insistence on quality and refinement in every detail. Rooms are equipped with an mp3 music player speaker stand and flat-screen television. The two "panoramic" suites have broad terraces with Eiffel Tower views. Light streams in through skylights running the length of the sitting room, and a wall of windows opens onto the terrace to create a contiguous indoor-outdoor living space. If light, space, and serenity have become the ultimate urban luxuries, de Sers has met the challenge.

RESTAURANT
GINGER

11, rue de Trémoille, 75008

Tel.: 01 47 23 37 32

Closed Saturday and Sunday.

Elegant Indochinese eatery offers spicy respite from conventional norms of the golden triangle neighborhood. Shady, contemporary Asiatic interior and attentive service.

BOUTIQUE—LINENS AND DECORATIVE OBJECTS
NOUEZ MOI (LILLIAN PONS-SEGUIN)

8, rue Clément Marot, 75008

Tel.: 01 47 20 60 26

Resolutely BCBG selection of gift items, linens, tablewear, and decorative objects with consideration for babies, hunters, and gatherers. Perfect place to pick up house gifts for a weekend in Sologne.

BOUTIQUE—WOMENSWEAR AND MENSWEAR
HOBBS CASHMERE

45, rue Pierre Charron, 75008

Tel.: 01 47 20 83 22

The royal seal on the facade is British, but the taste is French. For a quarter of a century, their luxe collection of Italian, French, and Scottish cashmeres have remained a birthday wish list staple.

HAIR AND BEAUTY SALON
LA BIOSTHÉTIQUE

35, avenue Pierre 1er de Serbie, 75008

Tel.: 01 56 64 03 10

Holistic hair care and beauty treatments pioneered in the early 1950s by biochemist Marcel Contier. The salon offers diagnostic hair and skin treatments including hair color, permanents, and makeup.

MASSAGE/WELLNESS
CENTRE ÉLYSÉE 63

63, avenue des Champs-Élysées, 75008

Tel.: 01 56 88 27 88 | www.elysee63.com | info@elysee63.com

Nirvana is now at this new-generation spa founded by alternative treatment guru Jean-Michel Eté and American businesswoman Tracy Posner with backing from Sting and Trudie Styler. Antoine Klam designed the exotic arts and crafts interior for optimum harmony. A to Z holistic treatments including reflexology, acupuncture, shiatsu massage, detox, and Indian Ayurvedic reinforced with yoga and pilates.

OPPOSITE CLOCKWISE FROM TOP LEFT:

French doors open onto a balcony with
a Pantheon view, Grands Hommes.

Wine labels featuring guest-room
paintings, Pont Royal.

Marcel Proust suite,
Relais Saint Germain.

Literary

GRANDS HOMMES
(5th), Panthéon
Privileged location by the Panthéon

PONT ROYAL
(7th), Saint-Germain
Left Bank intellectual landmark

RELAIS SAINT-GERMAIN
(6th), Odéon
Gourmet guest house with a taste for literature

Paris readily seduces visitors with the siren call of fashion, gastronomy, art, and architecture, but it also boasts a remarkable intellectual heritage. The historic center of letters and learning is concentrated on the Left Bank between the Latin Quarter and Saint-Germain. The 5th arrondissement, where Hôtel des Grands Hommes overlooks the Panthéon, includes the Sorbonne, Panthéon, historic lycées, and *grandes écoles*. Saint-Germain in the 6th has the densest concentration of publishers and bookstores in the city and is the perennial favored haunt of writers, philosophers, editors, artists, and intellectuals of every stripe, as well as home to the French Institute, where France's *éminences grises* are put out to pasture to update the dictionary in their golden years.

Pont Royal has an impressive literary pedigree, since its bar served as a meeting place for a generation of postwar Nobel laureates and literary upstarts. Though renowned for its cuisine, Relais Saint-Germain embodies the spirit of creative continuity. Chef-owner Yves Camdeborde recently authored a literary cookbook featuring anecdotes and recipes inspired by favorite authors.

GRANDS HOMMES

Privileged location by the Panthéon

Corinne Moncelli
17, place du Panthéon
75005 Paris
www.hoteldesgrandshommes.com

UCKILY THE GRANDS HOMMES became a hotel residence in the eighteenth century, because commercial real estate is visibly absent on place du Panthéon, one of the capital's most august civic spaces. Only Hotel Crillon on place de la Concorde has such elegant squatting rights on hallowed turf. Ringing the Panthéon is France's most prestigious *lycée*—Henri IV, the *mairie* (or town hall) of the fifth arrondissement, a law school, historic church, and neo-Renaissance library with an exterior frieze inscribed with names of notable scholars. In such company, the hotel is mindful of cultivating a suitably sober image, and throughout its history it has played host to professors, jurists, ministers, and the occasional Nobel Prize winner, who appreciate its proximity to the Sorbonne and Grandes Écoles. In 1918, rooms 51 and 52 sheltered the "pope of surrealism," André Breton. The hotel became headquarters for the nascent movement, and it was here that the revue *Littérature* was founded and Breton invented "automatic writing" with Philippe Soupault, who is credited with the anthem of every rebel spirit, "When one is young, it's for life."

In 2001, twenty years after her parents purchased Grands Hommes, current owner Corinne Moncelli took over management and has overseen a complete refurbishment. The fresh Directoire-style interior is in keeping with the building's architecture and a perfect complement to the elegant period stairwell. The main-floor décor is more formal and rigorously neoclassical than that of the guest rooms, where decorator Vincent Bastide leavens Napoleon's penchant for neoclassic imperialist symbolism with Josephine's fondness for bright color and floral motifs in a tasteful mélange of sobriety and whimsy. The only departure from the theme is the breakfast room situated in the former cellar, with characteristic exposed stone from foundations that predate the building above.

The choicest rooms, like 21, have French doors opening onto a balcony, where breakfast can be served. Room 61 offers a spectacular panorama. As is appropriate for an intellectual address, many guest rooms have a substantial writing desk destined to inspire journal entries. The desk in suite 31 is appropriate for a visiting minister or CEO but is also just fine for writing postcards. A ground-floor suite, which offers privacy and autonomy, is much in demand. Since the square is very

OPPOSITE:
Guest room with coordinating toile de Jouy wall paper and bed canopy.

ABOVE, FROM LEFT:
Guest room doors
have brass door
knocker fixtures.

This medallion frieze
is one of the many
decorative motifs with
a neoclassical theme.

Catch up on French news
in the daily *Le Figaro*.

OPPOSITE TOP:
Marble urn filled with
orchids and trailing
ivy, entry hall.

OPPOSITE BOTTOM LEFT:
Bedrooms feature historic
reproduction wall paper.

OPPOSITE BOTTOM RIGHT:
Cosy corner nook with
day bed sofa.

large, rooms across the front of the building benefit from an unusual degree of unobstructed light and air.

What most recommends the hotel is the unique location at the historic heart of French academia. The magnificent Luxembourg Gardens are just down avenue Soufflot (which leads off the *place*), and rue Mouffetard, one of the liveliest market streets in Paris, is a brief stroll in the other direction. Hemingway, better known for carousing and skirt chasing than pursuit of advanced degrees, spent his *Moveable Feast* years in a cramped apartment around the corner on rue du Cardinal Lemoine and frequented cafés around place de la Contrescarpe—the perennial meeting place for students and the backpacking youth hostel crowd.

Grands Hommes has a ringside seat overlooking the towering Panthéon, which was the highest building in Paris until it was overtaken by the Eiffel Tower. The austere edifice housing the tombs of France's "great men" is vaguely modeled after the Roman Pantheon. Originally commissioned by Louis XV to replace the ruined church of St. Genevieve, dedicated to the city's patron saint, the intervening revolution repositioned the unfinished project as a secular monument and the designs were finalized by a pupil of the by-then-deceased Soufflot.

Despite the name of the hotel, two women keep company with the likes of Voltaire, Victor Hugo, Émile Zola, Louis Braille, and de Gaulle's culture minister André Malraux under the Panthéon's dome. Marie Curie earned a place on merit, while another woman worked out a deal to join her venerated husband. It is certainly worth a visit to test your knowledge of French history. More than a few of these national heroes walked the pavements of the neighborhood and would have known Hotel des Grands Hommes, which is why it's an address that continues to resonate among French intellectuals.

RESTAURANT
LE COSI

9, rue Cujas, 75005
Tel.: 01 43 29 20 20 | www.le-cosi.com
Monday–Saturday.
A cheerfully appointed Corsican bistro run by a duo of twenty-something natives serving what food critic Patricia Wells labels "a perfect blend of country French and Italian." Try the smoked pork and sheep's-milk cheesecake.

GOURMET FOOD—CHARCUTERIE
CHARCUTERIE DU PANTHÉON–
M. ET MME. JEAN-FRANÇOIS KOLANO

200, rue Saint-Jacques, 75005
Tel.: 01 43 54 24 48
Nostalgia-inducing Old World charcuterie on a timeless Parisian market street. The homemade mashed potatoes are highly recommended.

MUSEUM
MUSÉE NATIONAL DU MOYEN AGE (NATIONAL MUSEUM OF THE MIDDLE AGES—THE BATHS AND HÔTEL DE CLUNY)

6, place Paul Painlevé, 75005
Tel.: 01 53 73 78 00 | www.musee-moyenage.fr
Open daily, 9:15 A.M.–5:45 P.M.; closed Tuesday.
A museum within a double landmark encompassing remarkably preserved second-century Gallo-Roman baths and a fifteenth-century abbatial palace. The extensive collection of medieval treasures includes the much-reproduced *Lady with the Unicorn* tapestry.

LANDMARK
LES ARÈNES DE LUTÈCE

Rue de Navarre and 49, rue Monge, 75005
Monday–Friday, 8 A.M.–9 P.M.; Saturday, Sunday, and holidays, 9 A.M.–9 P.M.
Free entry
Vestige of the Gallo-Roman city center uncovered in 1869 while Haussmann was excavating a new road. The amphitheater, built to accommodate fifteen thousand, is now a peaceful neighborhood park until school lets out and the ball kickers move in.

WINE BAR RESTAURANT
CAFÉ DE LA NOUVELLE MAIRIE

19–21, rue des Fossés Saint Jacques, 75005
Tel.: 01 44 07 04 41
Monday–Friday, 9 A.M.–10 P.M.; Tuesday and Thursday until 11 P.M.
Reputable natural wine bar offering of over a dozen vintages by the glass and a blackboard specials bistro menu. Youthful staff, relaxed ambiance, and Parisian clientele including local academics.

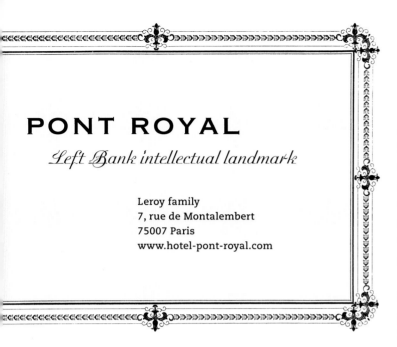

PONT ROYAL

Left Bank intellectual landmark

Leroy family
7, rue de Montalembert
75007 Paris
www.hotel-pont-royal.com

OPPOSITE:
Joël Robuchon's two star
L'Atelier restaurant caters
room service for the hotel.

$\mathcal{R}$EVOLUTIONARY ART MAY HAVE CEASED to germinate in Montparnasse ateliers and literary lions no longer prowl the bars and cafés of Saint-Germain, but their ghosts have left a potent trail on the Left Bank, witness to so many breakthrough twentieth-century artistic and literary movements. Few Saint-Germain landmarks rival the accreditation of Pont Royal, which served as dormitory and watering hole for a generation of artists and intellectuals.

In her forward to *Paris*, written by her art critic husband John Russell, Rosamond Bernier, founder of avant-garde 1950s art magazine *L'OEIL,* reminisced about living at the hotel during its postwar heyday: "The painter Balthus, more Byronic than Byron himself, would drop by and give me news of Picasso. Jean-Paul Sartre and Simone de Beauvoir were regulars...they had abandoned their previous headquarters at the Café Flore for the less exposed Pont-Royal."

What remains unchanged is an ace location straddling the 6th and 7th off rue du Bac and unparallelled views from the upper floors. Bernier described the vista from her top-floor nest as "Paris in my pocket." Standing on a balcony, you see clear up rue du Bac, across the Seine and Louvre on to Sacré Coeur, with Invalides, Grand Palais, and the Eiffel Tower visible with a mere turn of the head. The double terrace of the Panoramic Penthouse is the place to enjoy sunset on a balmy June evening with a flute of Champagne.

The Leroy family considers Pont Royal the jewel in the crown of their select group of Parisian hotels. After purchasing the 1923 building in 1997, Robert Leroy shut it for a two-year renovation. It reemerged far more polished, with a retro-style décor by Alain Marcot. A stone plaque to the right of the entrance is inscribed "Hôtel Littéraire," and the sleek circular lobby is rimmed with vintage photographs of notable personalities and Nobel laureates who congregated there. The theme is continued along upstairs corridors, with framed reproductions of letters and drawings by writers and artists.

The Pont Royal has the luxury of several reception rooms, a rarity for a hotel of its size. In keeping with tradition, the clubby Signature bar is open daily from 11 a.m. to midnight. The book-filled Salon Vélin is stylishly Parisian with hunter-green-and-bordeaux striped fabric-covered walls, coordinating club chairs, a

OPPOSITE LEFT:
The Salon Vélin is an
elegant refuge for a quiet
after-dinner drink.

OPPOSITE RIGHT,
TOP TO BOTTOM:
Lobby rotunda
photo frieze of literary
personalities.

Guest room overlooking
stained-glass window
of St Thomas d'Aquin.

Breakfast table
overlooking zen
garden.

OVERLEAF:
View up rue du Bac
across the Seine, the
Louvre, and on to Sacré
Coeur in Montmartre from
a top-floor room.

green ceramic stove, and an artful hanging of Asiatic prints. This is the room to book for a private dinner with friends catered by "chef of the century" Joël Robuchon's l'Atelier restaurant next door. Though the two establishments are independent, the hotel has a privileged relationship with one of the most coveted tables in Paris, and there is a private entrance to the restaurant from the hotel lobby. The 2008 Michelin red guide awarded it a second star, making it the only restaurant of its grade with counter service.

A no-reservations policy increases the challenge of getting a table, but Pont Royal has the unique option of ordering room service from the menu during l'Atelier's lunch and dinner hours. The restaurant also oversees breakfast served in the hotel's Mosaique garden room, where daylight streams in from four skylights and a wall of windows overlooking a Japanese garden.

In celebration of the relaunch, the owners commissioned a series of paintings so that each guest room would have an original artwork hanging above the bed. Students at the École des Beaux-Arts were asked to create works taking the Pont Royal (bridge) as inspiration. Since the family is also proprietor of Château Barateau, an Haut-Médoc vineyard, the paintings were reproduced on wine labels, and the collection of bottles is on display in a case off the central lobby.

Several rooms on the back side of the hotel have exceptional views of a church that abuts the building. The windows of room 611 are perfectly positioned for admiring the semicircular top of an impressive stained-glass window. Mahogany-paneled guest rooms are thoroughly equipped with stylish built in bar, two direct-line phones, high-speed internet access and satellite television, as one would expect in a hotel that prides itself on service. From management down, the staff is highly professional, and the concierge service is the equal of far larger establishments, making the Pont Royal a good choice for visitors who are new to Paris, appreciate help implementing their itinerary, or those who simply wish to benefit from one of the city's choicest locations.

GOURMET FOOD—CHEESE

ANDROUET

37, rue de Verneuil, 75007

Tel.: 01 42 61 97 55

Tuesday–Saturday, Monday afternoon.

Family-run cheese merchant reputed to be the best in the city and soon to celebrate its hundredth anniversary. This is one of five outlets.

RESTAURANT

GAYA RIVE GAUCHE—PAR PIERRE GAGNAIRE

44, rue du Bac, 75007

Tel.: 01 45 44 73 73 | www.pierregagnaire.com/francais/cdgaia.htm

Gagnaire opened this "simple" fish restaurant to show what he can do on a pared-down scale with a minimum of fuss. The contemporary gray-and-blue interior is as refreshing as the astutely prepared fresh produce.

BOUTIQUE—CURIOSITY/ZOOLOGY AND HORTICULTURE

DEYROLLE

46, rue du Bac, 75007

Tel.: 01 42 22 30 07 | www.deyrolle.fr

On February 1, 2008, a fire ripped through the taxidermy and insect exhibits on the upper floor destroying a collection that has attracted visitors since 1831. Donations from regional museums and private collectors, backed up by fundraising efforts including an Hermès scarf and Christie's auction, should enable entrepreneurial owner *"prince jardinier"* Louis Albert de Broglie to restore the landmark to its former splendor.

RESTAURANT

BISTRO DE PARIS

33, rue de Lille, 75007

Tel.: 01 42 61 16 83

Antidote to the somewhat intimidating creativity of Robuchon and Gagnaire. This historic destination with its red-and-gold Belle Époque interior and predictable classic bistro dishes perpetuates the comforting familiarity of a certain Parisian ideal that seems resistant to the vagaries of fashion.

MUSEUM

MUSÉE MAILLOL–FONDATION DINA VIERNY

61, rue de Grenelle, 75007

Tel.: 01 42 22 59 58 | www.muséemaillol.com

contact@muséemaillol.com

A private museum in two parts, consecrated to the work of Maillol plus a permanent collection comprising important modern and contemporary works. Vierny, who became a gallery owner and passionate collector, was a model from the age of fifteen for Maillol and a source of inspiration for Matisse and Bonnard.

RELAIS SAINT-GERMAIN

*Gourmet guest house
with a taste for literature*

Claudine and Yves Camdeborde
9, carrefour de l'Odéon
75006 Paris
www.hotelrsg.com

CHEF YVES CAMDEBORDE knows that the surest way to establish rapport with hotel guests is to win them over with a meal. "Cuisine works magic; once I've fed guests, we've shared something and I find it easy to talk with them." He may be doing too good a job, since it's nearly impossible to get a dinner reservation at his hot gourmet bistro Le Comptoir without booking a room at the Relais Saint-Germain next door. This isn't a commercial ploy. In 2005 he and his wife, Claudine, moved on from a successful restaurant in the 14th to pursue their dream of creating a rural *pension de famille* in the city. Another of Camdeborde's passions is literature, so finding a boutique hotel in the epicenter of Saint-Germain with a historic bistro next door felt like destiny. Rimbaud and Paul Verlaine lived down the street on rue Monsieur le Prince, and Baudelaire on neighboring rue de Seine. Guest rooms at Relais Saint-Germain are named after legendary writers, and to celebrate the inextricable bond between literature and cuisine Camdeborde recently coauthored *Room Service*, a book of recipes created in homage to writers, from Proust to Hemingway, who share his love of food and Paris.

To apprentice with the best, Camdeborde migrated to Paris from Pau, where his father raised pigs and his mother ran a charcuterie. The bistro logo pays homage to the *cochon*, a Comptoir staple Camdeborde prepares with infinite versatility, from slices of Iberian ham carved right from the hock at breakfast, to potted pâtés served at lunch and delicate poached and roasted milk-fed pork on the gastronomic dinner menu. The pig insignia is also embroidered on polar fleece lap blankets provided at the sidewalk tables favored by smokers. Since the café and restaurant smoking ban took effect, heaters have been installed under the awning, which has also eased the midday rush, when reservations are not accepted.

After toiling in the pressure cooker of haute cuisine at the Ritz and Crillon, Camdeborde concluded that he craved intimacy and authenticity more than artifice and Michelin stars. He appreciates that a small-scale operation permits substantive relationships with staff, clients, and suppliers. In his youth Yves aspired to become a professional rugby player, and he runs his hotel and restaurant with the dynamism and dedication of a team captain. "On a sports team, every position is important for the success of the whole, and when the pressure is on you

OPPOSITE:
Secluded library stocked
with old and new editions.

136

OPPOSITE TOP, FROM LEFT:
Guest-room detail with antique tea jar and suite of silhouette prints.

Detail, painting in ground-floor ante room leading to the restaurant.

Upper-floor bathroom illuminated by a sky light.

Trompe l'oeil wood paneling is a craft-paper and ink illusion.

OPPOSITE BOTTOM:
Le Comptoir bistro set for breakfast.

OVERLEAF, RIGHT:
Coquettish Antoine Blondin suite with pillows trimmed in faux fur.

discover who gives up and who keeps fighting. It's the same dynamic in a kitchen, and I've learned from both experiences that you make the most progress in adversity." His staff is clearly dedicated and more than a little in awe of their boss's indefatigable curiosity and enthusiasm. The wine list reflects Camdeborde's advocacy of *vins du terroir*—small producers who chafe at uniformity and are in the vanguard of the return to natural vinification. "He wants to promote every region, renews his list frequently, and tries to provide discoveries for every budget" is how the barman describes Camdeborde's wine-selection strategy.

Stana, the hotel manager, has worked at the Relais since it opened under previous management more than twenty years ago. What she enjoys most about her job is the longstanding relationships she develops: "I like catching up with guests who return year after year and watching children grow up." She admits that first-timers are sometimes taken aback by the hotel's casual ambiance because it doesn't conform to their expectation of a four-star hotel, but after one night they appreciate the difference. For a start, room size is generous for the neighborhood and nothing is cookie-cutter about the décor. If a choice of rooms is available at check-in, you should request a tour, as style and color scheme vary considerably. Claudine Camdeborde has meticulously supervised the refurbishment of the guest rooms, appointing them with fine fabrics, antiques, and artwork collected over the years. Most rooms also have a selection of books, which is a rare amenity today. Another charming feature is the closet doors, which are built from old recuperated doors or paneling and exposed beams which testify to the building's seventeenth-century origins.

Rooms overlooking the *place* provide a glimpse of Parisian street life at one of the city's most picturesque crossroads. *Odéon* means "theater," and the scene viewed from rooms along the front of the hotel delivers on the promise. The Frédéric Dard room, on the second floor, and Margarite de Navarre, with a private terrace on the fifth floor, are lovely choices. Suites are good value, especially Carnosky, which has French windows with wrought-iron balustrades.

In a worthy tribute to Yves Camdeborde's uncompromising standards at every price point, a classic *jambon-beurre* baguette sandwich purchased in March 2008 from his Créperie du Comptoir takeout sandwich shop adjacent to the bistro was judged to be the finest in Paris in a blind taste test conducted by *Le Figaro*. So you can indulge in the rarity of a gourmet treat for three euros fifty in the privacy of your room.

YVES CAMDEBORDE'S COUPS DE COEUR

GALLERY—JEWELRY AND CRAFTS
GALERIE HÉLÈNE PORÉE
1, rue de l'Odéon, 75006
Tel.: 01 43 54 17 00 | www.galerie-helene-poree.com
Tuesday–Saturday, 11 A.M.–1 P.M. and 2 P.M.–7 P.M.
Arts and crafts dealer with a refined aesthetic exhibiting ceramics, glass, and contemporary jewelry by French and international artists.

BOUTIQUE—KNIVES AND CUTLERY
CECCALDI
15, rue Racine, 75006
Tel.: 01 46 33 87 20 | www.coueaux-ceccaldi.com
Pocket and carving knives plus elegant tableware hand forged in Corsica representing the best in traditional French craftsmanship. Camdeborde is a fan of the wood-handled carving knives.

BOOKSELLER AND EDITOR
LE DILETTANTE
19, rue Racine, 75006
Tel.: 01 43 37 98 98 | www.ledilettante.com
Monday–Saturday, 10:30 A.M.–7 P.M.
An immersion in history and literature. Specializes in twentieth-century authors and is also an independent publisher.

FLORIST
PASCAL MUTEL
6, carrefour de l'Odéon, 75006
Tel.: 01 43 26 02 56
Mutel met the challenge of taking over Christian Tortu's renowned shop. They share a similar spirit, but Mutel has his own signature style.

BOUTIQUE—WOMENSWEAR AND ACCESSORIES
KYRIE ELEISON
15, carrefour de l'Odéon, 75006
Tel.: 01 46 34 26 91 | studio@kyrieeleison.fr
The warm manner and astute eye of the two young owners makes shopping here a treat. With a little guidance, Camdeborde says, he is sure to select the perfect surprise for his wife.

Contemporary art

LE A
(8th), *Faubourg Saint-Honoré*
A-typical elegance

DES ACADEMIES ET DES ARTS
(6th), *Montparnasse*
Echoes of les *Années Folles*

HÔTEL PARTICULIER MONTMARTRE
(18th), *Rue Lepic*
Installations in a Directoire mansion

NOAILLES
(2nd), *Opéra*
Zen à la française at city center

The Contemporary Art group includes four destinations where artistic creation is a focal point rather than a decorative feature. The hotel owners are enthusiastic collectors who either showcase their personal collections or commissioned site-specific work by established and emerging artists. The hotels feature art created by living French artists working in a range of mediums and styles from figurative painting to conceptual installation, photography, and video.

At Le A, Des Académies et des Arts, and Hôtel Particulier Montmartre, artists either painted or applied their work directly onto interior and exterior walls or created sculptures and installations for guest rooms and communal spaces.

Appropriately, Des Académies et des Arts is located in Montmartre and Hôtel Particulier in Montparnasse, two Parisian neighborhoods synonymous with bohemian communities where impressionist and modernist masters from Renoir and Utrillo to Modigliani and Picasso lived and worked.

LE A

A-typical elegance

Sorman family
4, rue d'Artois
75008 Paris
www.hotel-le-a-paris.com

*I*F THERE'S A PARISIAN *quartier* needing an oasis of tranquility, it's the 8th arrondissement business district between the Champs-Élysées and Faubourg Saint-Honoré. Happily, an enlightened private hotel group transformed one of their properties into a Zen refuge at the eye of the storm, a place where guests can decompress beside a fireplace amid shelves lined with hundreds of contemporary art and design books. "A," pronounced "ahh" in French, takes on new meaning.

The hotel's originality owes credit to the creative freedom permitted interior designer Frédéric Méchiche and artist Fabrice Hybert. Gigi Sorman, who supervised the project, encouraged innovation, if not eccentricity, so everyone might feel at home. The hotel's transformation is in step with the Champs-Élysées renaissance, which thanks to an aesthetic crackdown has recovered cachet as a prestigious address.

The creative team had carte blanche, since a gut renovation preserved only the classic Haussmann-era facade and a nineteenth-century *verrière* now covering the breakfast room and bar. Méchiche, who is best known for residential commissions, welcomed this commercial project because he was able to give art the central role he does in a private home rather than treat it as mere decoration. His graphic décor complements Hybert's poetic and whimsical work. Hybert, whose French Pavilion at the 1997 Venice Biennale won the coveted Leone d'Oro, created work for the hotel in unexpected mediums from tapestry to light diodes. The twenty-six guest rooms feature an original drawing previewed in a miniature sketch next to each door. The mood of his charcoal-and-mixed media drawings ranges from minimalist to ebullient, and images frequently incorporate wordplay.

Méchiche uses custom black and white furnishings accented with brushed metal and ebony wood to compose elegant interior spaces. Signature pieces include tubular suspended lamps, tailored armchairs slipcovered in pristine white, groupings of tall frosted glass vases, and striped carpet and tiling suggestive of the graphic art of Daniel Buren, renowned for his Palais Royal installation of black-and-white striped columns.

The impeccable slipcovers (changed for each guest) and flawless white piqué bedding give guest rooms a starched freshness. Despite the busy character of the neighborhood, double double-glazed windows ensure that tranquility reigns within.

OPPOSITE:
White slipcovers are changed for each guest to ensure a pristine welcome.

OPPOSITE:

The lounge's open fireplace, ebony-stained oak floor, plus velvet and leather upholstery create a cozy chalet atmosphere

ABOVE, FROM LEFT:

Fabrice Hybert's woodland tapestry mural, bar room.

Bathroom tiling in designer Frédéric Méchice's trademark contrasting stripes.

Cord-free suspended lanterns replace bedside and floor fixtures.

While light-infused guest rooms have a graphic elegance, the ground-floor library lounge and breakfast room and bar exude subtle drama. The walls of the breakfast room are hung with a floor-to-ceiling tapestry featuring tree trunks in a dense forest, and an exterior wall visible through the skylight is decorated with myriad renditions of the letter "A" painted in molten glass on Mexican ceramic tiles. The lounge library has a cozy chalet ambiance enhanced by a fireplace inset into a wall, ebony-stained oak plank floor, chocolate velvet upholstered couches, and leather armchairs. Hyber uses imaginative lighting in the elevator to fanciful effect (the color shifts at each floor), and hallways are dimly lit, in keeping with a twilight trend in contemporary hotels.

Clientele includes a healthy percentage of creative types—writers, artists, designers, media, and fashion professionals—who appreciate the novelty of a chic guest-house ambiance in a business neighborhood. Emma Charles, recruited from the prestigious Four Seasons hotel chain to manage Le A, is mindful of the importance of personalized service. She sees herself as a *maîtresse de la maison* whose duty it is to anticipate the needs of her clientele. "Guests appreciate a haven of peace in the midst of so much effervescence. They like being greeted by a familiar face and tell me they come back because they feel at home." Emma's rituals include personalized notes and afternoon tea in the lounge to encourage visitors to relax and recuperate before launching into a busy evening.

There is something delightfully French about the synergy of fashion and culture pervading Le A. The imaginative décor succeeds in being unexpected without teetering into ostentation or special effects. At chez A, less is more, a hallmark of Parisian style.

EMMA CHARLES'S COUPS DE COEUR

RARE-BOOK AUCTION HOUSE
ARTCURIAL
7, Rond-Point des Champs-Élysées, 75008

Tel.: 01 42 99 20 20 | www.artcurial.com | contact@artcurial.com

Bibliophile paradise. Artcurial specializes in engraved and illustrated books, limited and first editions, and the revered art of *bandes dessinées* (comic strips). If you are hankering for a Rimbaud *Season in Hell* original edition or a *Tintin* signed by Hergé, this is where you could get lucky.

TEA SALON
LADURÉE CHAMPS-ÉLYSÉES
75, avenue des Champs-Élysées, 75008

Tel.: 01 40 75 08 75 | www.ladurée.fr

Boutique: weekdays, 7:30 A.M.–11:00 P.M.; Saturday, 8:30 A.M.–midnight; Sunday, 8:30 A.M.–10 P.M. Restaurant: daily, 7:30 A.M.–12:30 A.M.

Über designer Jacques Garcia has created a confectionary boudoir for savoring the famed macaroons (in forty flavors), *marrons glacés*, hand-made chocolates, and ice cream.

BAR RESTAURANT
LE BRISTOL
112, rue du Faubourg Saint-Honoré, 75008

Tel.: 01 53 43 43 00 | www.hotel-bristol.com

Less formal than the main restaurant but every bit as chic. Open for lunch, a light dinner, or afternoon tea and pastries.

HEALTH AND BEAUTY
CARITA MAISON DE BEAUTÉ
11, rue Faubourg Saint-Honoré, 75008

Tel.: 01 44 94 11 11 | www.maisondebeautecarita.fr

House of beauty founded by the ground-breaking Carita sisters, who remain a reference in the salon world. Hair, face, and body are accorded equal attention.

RESTAURANT
MARKET
15, avenue Matignon, 75008

Tel.: 01 56 43 40 90

Lunch and dinner; closed Sunday.

Jean-George Vongerichten's first Parisian restaurant is a joint venture with film director Luc Besson and François Pinault. The Frenchman from New York registered a hit in a fast-paced business and shopping district with inventive gastronomic fusion cuisine and a faultlesslessly elegant Christian Liagre–designed setting.

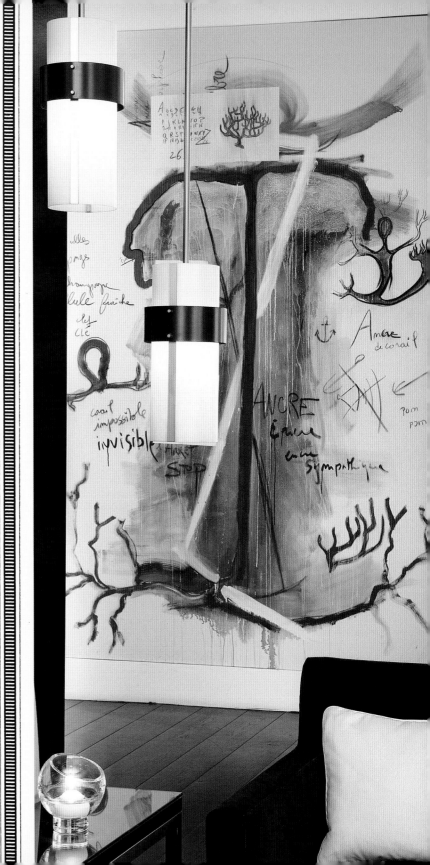

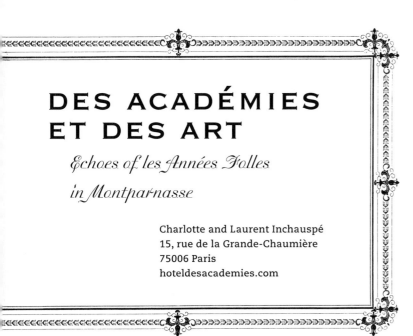

DES ACADÉMIES ET DES ART

Echoes of les Années Folles in Montparnasse

Charlotte and Laurent Inchauspé
15, rue de la Grande-Chaumière
75006 Paris
hoteldesacademies.com

RUE DE LA GRANDE CHAUMIÈRE, off boulevard du Montparnasse, is a mythic address in the history of modern art. The legend was launched in 1880 with the opening of Colarossi's, the first professional art school in the quarter, and by the 1920s, when Montparnasse was a colony of international artists and writers, the street housed four schools, as many art supply shops, and the headquarters of the Artist's Union and Artist's Federation. Modigliani's and Gauguin's studios were at number 8, Strindberg lodged at number 12, and the bohemian crowd congregated at Chez Charlotte, where the patron had an eye for emerging talent and would barter meals for art or extend credit to struggling creatives.

All that remains of the former Hôtel des Académies at number 15 is the original wrought-iron-and-glass marquee with retro signage marking the entrance, but the new owners are perpetuating its heritage through a collaboration with French contemporary artists whose work is integrated within the new interior.

In the spring of 2007 Charlotte and Laurent Inchauspé left careers as a music journalist and a film producer to collaborate on a project they could call their own. After a year's renovation they reopened Des Académies et des Arts in March 2008. Charlotte, responsible for the design concept, engaged painter Jérôme Mesnager and sculptor Sophie de Watrigant, two artists whose work features stylized white human figures, to create customized pieces. Mesnager's androgynous jointed figures have become familiar silhouettes in urban spaces around the world since he emerged among a generation of graffiti artists in the 1980s.

In guest rooms Mesnager painted directly onto canvas fabric wall coverings. Two large public-space installations reflect his penchant for surprise. A giant figure stretches the height of a five-story wall of the interior courtyard and a ride in the glass-backed elevator reveals figures scaling the wall of the shaft. De Watrigant's diminutive modeled figures evocatively posed on ladders are displayed throughout ground-floor reception rooms and most dramatically on a metallic rope ladder running up the central stairwell.

In collaboration with architect Vincent Bastille, Charlotte chose four design themes inspired by personalities and styles from the Roaring Twenties for the twenty guest rooms—Man Ray, Ruhlmann, Comédienne, and Parisienne.

OPPOSITE:
A jubilant Jérôme Mesnager mural frames a stone fireplace in the reception sitting room.

150

OPPOSITE TOP:
Books and photos in the library feature celebrated Montparnasse artists.

BOTTOM LEFT:
Detail, leather-upholstered booth in video projection room.

OPPOSITE BOTTOM RIGHT:
Oversize tufted-velvet headboard in the *Comédienne* room.

An homage to photography and Man Ray is the most graphic, featuring subtle gradations of gray and beige contrasted with black and white. Blackout curtains separating bed and bathrooms are a clever darkroom pun.

Parisienne-theme rooms have views onto the inner courtyard and Mesnager's giant wall mural. The color scheme is a sophisticated mix of cream, taupe, and burgundy with touches of aubergine crushed velvet. Since coquettish *Parisiennes* love to shop, the wardrobe is especially commodious. The roomy Ruhlmann is a paean to a design master of *les Années Folles*. Frosted-glass-and-chrome wall sconces, a chenille bedspread, and deco-inspired pewter satin upholstered vanity stool create a streamlined, soigné ambiance.

The playful *Comédienne* room evokes the stages of rue de la Gaîté with red drapes, an oversize headboard upholstered in tufted ruby velvet, violet carpeting, and scarlet armchairs.

Guest-room doors inset with panels of smoked glass add a dimension of light and space to corridors. Convenience features including an electronic "do not disturb" button, dimmer switches, wall- or furniture-mounted phones, and reading lights all reflect consideration for amenities that enhance guests' enjoyment of their stay.

The layout of the ground floor with one room flowing into the next around the perimeter of the building makes optimal use of space. Large picture windows on the street side provide plenty of natural light. The reception sitting room has a plush sofa and elegant chocolate and gunmetal leather armchairs on either side of a carved stone fireplace framed by a Mesnager mural on distressed wood panelling. To the left of the entrance is a reposeful library with a selection of art and design books on the major cultural figures of Montparnasse from Picasso to Man Ray muse Kiki.

Beyond the library is the clandestine *petit bistro*. Running the length of the back wall is a skylit video screening room with banquettes and sleek white tables, where guests can view art videos while eating breakfast. Chairs in the courtyard are the same design as those found in neighboring Luxembourg gardens.

Massage services are available upon request in a wellness center deliciously perfumed with a pungent Dyptique candle created by John Galliano. In all, Des Académies et des Arts is one of the most luxurious and intimate three-star destinations in the city.

LAURENT INCHAUSPÉ'S COUPS DE COEUR

RESTAURANT
LE TIMBRE
3, rue Saint-Beuve, 75006
Tel.: 01 45 49 10 40 | www.restaurantletimbre.com
Closed Sunday and Monday.
Adorable twenty-seat bistro where the kitchen opens onto the dining room. Wonderful French dishes cooked up by an Englishman. A neighborhood favorite.

RESTAURANT
WADJA
10, rue de la Grande-Chaumière, 75006
Tel.: 01 46 33 02 02 Closed Sunday, and Monday lunch.
Bistro run by chef with a haute cuisine résumé serving a choice of hearty and healthful dishes. Daily specials are good value.

LATE-NIGHT BAR
LE ROSEBUD
11 bis, rue Delambre, 75014
Tel.: 01 43 35 38 54 Open daily, 7 P.M.–2 A.M.
Tuxedo-clad staff serves up classic cocktails in a soigné Montparnassian whiskey bar right out of a bygone era where artists and intellectuals continue to gather.

ART AND CULTURE
FONDATION CARTIER
261, boulevard Raspail, 75014
Tel.: 01 42 18 56 50 | www.fondation.cartier.com
Open daily, 11 A.M.–8 P.M., Tuesday until 10 P.M.; closed Monday.
Since 1984 the Cartier foundation for contemporary art has been promoting living international artists. The collection includes over three hundred works by a hundred artists.

ART AND CULTURE
MUSÉE ZADKINE
100 bis, rue d'Assas, 75006
Tel.: 01 55 42 77 20 | www.zadkine.paris.fr
Open daily, 10 A.M.–6 P.M.; closed Monday and holidays.
Residence and atelier from 1928 until his death in 1967 of expat Russian master whose sculpture evolved from reflecting the modern influence of primitive art and cubism to the development of a personal vernacular integrating man and nature. A program of contemporary art exhibitions and cultural events augments the museum.

HÔTEL PARTICULIER MONTMARTRE

Installations in a Directoire mansion

Morgane Rousseau
23, avenue Junot
75018 Paris
www.hotel-particulier-mont-
martre.com

OPPOSITE:
Surrounded by a lush
walled garden, Hôtel
Particulier is an ultra-
private retreat.

*A*VENUE JUNOT IS ONE OF THE CITY'S loveliest residential street. Add to that its location in one of Paris's best-preserved neighborhoods and you have an exceptional destination. Removed from neon Pigalle and touristy Sacré Coeur, Hôtel Particulier Montmartre sits between an authentic windmill and private *boules* club, in an enclave where one can still envision a young Edith Piaf singing on the corner.

In the nineteenth century, bourgeois families built country homes here amid hillside vineyards and dozens of windmills. As urbanization encroached, the fringe district become notorious for cabarets, dance halls, ramshackle wooden cabins, and bohemian residents. Avenue Junot was carved out of the hillside in 1910 as part of an urban plan for cleaning up the Maquis shantytown. From the 1920s until the outbreak of World War II, it developed as a showplace for contemporary homes by avant-garde architects including Austrian master Adolf Loos, whose sole French project is a 1926 home he designed for writer Tristan Tzara and his wife, the painter Knitson, which abuts the hotel.

Hôtel Particulier Montmartre is reached via a private lane linking avenue Junot to rue Lepic. The entry is marked by a folly known as Witch's Rock—a naturalistic sculpture created by impressionist Felix Ziem, who had the distinction of being the only artist of his generation to be exhibited at the Louvre in his lifetime. The residence is hidden behind an imposing gate but once buzzed in you enter an idyllic garden shaded by improbably tall trees with a path leading to a handsome mansion. First impressions are somewhat misleading, as the current owners have animated the traditional building with the work of contemporary French artists. Owner Morgane Rousseau is an art insider, having created a program of artist residencies and exhibitions at Château de Bionnay in the Beaujolais. For her latest project she invited several artists who resided at Bionnay to collaborate in the decoration of the hotel's five themed suites.

The Directoire building, a former residence of the Guerrand-Hermès family, was already impeccably modernized when Rousseau acquired it in 2006. The previous owner installed an elevator and lavish bathrooms (several with a Jacuzzi and steam room) and commissioned the revered landscape artist Louis Bénech (who redesigned the Tuileries gardens by the Louvre) to create a garden that remains in

OPPOSITE, FROM LEFT:
Detail of colorized photographic treescape imagery, suite 4.

Elegantly appointed bathroom, suite 4.

An open-ended bathroom is a transitional space within the *Arbres à Oreilles* suite.

Room service breakfast, Hats and Poetry suite.

BOTTOM:
The salon is furnished with modern design classics easily rearranged in myriad seating formations.

OVERLEAF:
Neo-art nouveau *Arbre à Oreilles* suite by Pierre Fichefeux.

bloom year round. Rousseau describes the house as a structure with relatively few rooms but large volumes.

An eclectic melding of edgy art, *brocante* finds, and elegant interior design sets Hôtel Particulier Montmartre apart from conventional *hôtels de charme* and has made it a hit with the film, art, and fashion set. The mood of the spacious suites ranges from the whimsical haberdashery chic of curator Olivier Sallard's Hats and Poetry Suite to the richly hued woodland photomontage dreamscape of romantic Suite Four overlooking the front garden. Being French contemporary art, intellectual and conceptual executions predominate with winks at Magritte, surrealism, and dada. She limited each artist's contribution to a specific intervention in each suite while she focused on guests' needs and material comfort. Daylight streams throughout second-floor guest rooms and, with windows open and the trees in leaf, the view creates a delightful impression of being perched in a tree house.

The clever layout and sumptuousness of the bathrooms is an added aesthetic and sensual treat. A window in the ravishing spring-green bathroom of Suite Four overlooks a *boules* club, whose members chained themselves to trees when the city threatened to demolish it to construct an underground parking lot. The membership won out, and the city was obliged to restore the picturesque site—which has become a pride of the neighborhood.

The salon extending across the length of the ground floor is decidedly modern. Oversize contemporary photographs, furnishing classics by Le Corbusier and Joe Columbo, a graphic pony-skin rug, and contemporary art and design books create a cool lounge ambiance. The room is divided into three distinct seating areas for maximum privacy, and guests are encouraged to use the self-service bar. A collection of art books and DVDs is available in the adjoining library reception, where the fireplace is lit in cool months. The atmosphere makes you feel like a privileged houseguest, and the salon is well configured for scheduling an informal meeting or gathering of friends for a predinner cocktail. Guests are provided a set of house keys for returning in the wee hours.

In fair weather, breakfast is served on a verdant terrace off the garden-level dining room. A chef is available to prepare lunch or dinner (with twenty-four-hours' notice) in the ecclesiastically themed dining room with red-and-gold damask tablecloth, extravagant candelabras, and a beneficent guardian angel camouflaged amid plush red velvet drapes.

In short, this is a privileged address that synthesizes the charm of historic and hip, town and country in an arrondissement encompassing the spirit of Paris.

BOUTIQUE—WOMENSWEAR, LUGGAGE, AND ACCESSORIES

ORLA KIELY

4, rue Tholozé, 75018

Tel.: 01 42 54 28 08 | www.orlakiely.com

Tuesday–Saturday, 10:30 A.M.–7:30 P.M.

This UK designer's line of clothing and accessories, suitcases, and housewares is distinguished by graphic print fabrics in subtle color combinations. Quality and practicality are her signature traits.

MUSEUM

MUSÉE DE MONTMARTRE

12, rue Cortot, 75018

Tel.: 01 49 25 89 37 | infos@museedemontmarte.fr

Tuesday–Sunday, 11 A.M.–6 P.M.

Not every Paris neighborhood has a museum, because few have as colorful a history to commemorate, nor a working vineyard. The museum and cultural center occupies the oldest residential building on the butte, which once housed the studios of Renoir, Dufy, and Utrillo. The current exhibition, in collaboration with the absinthe museum in Auvers, documents Montmartre's affiliation with the infamous "green fairy."

LANDMARK

MONTMARTRE CEMETERY

Rue Caulaincourt, 75018

Père Lachaise may lure the Doors fans, but there are some distinguished plots here amid twenty acres of mossy paths shaded by chestnut trees, including those of Nijinsky, Dumas, Dégas, Zola, Truffaut, Stendhal, Guitry, and Berlioz.

CABARET

AU LAPIN AGILE

22, rue des Saules, 75018

Tel.: 01 46 06 85 87

Tuesday–Sunday, 9 P.M.–2 A.M.

A hundred years on, talent is still auditioning to hone their art before a small audience eager to discover the next great humorist, singer, or poet.

LANDMARK

CHÂTEAU DES BROUILLARDS

Allée des Brouillards (13, rue Girardon), 75018

Legend has it that Saint Denis was martyred here and carried his severed head to the outskirts of the city (where his basilica stands) before collapsing. The eighteenth-century mansion erected on the site was home to painter Pierre-Auguste Renoir in the 1890s and inspired the eponymous 1932 novel by Roland Dorgelès.

NOAILLES

Zen à la française at city center

Martine Falck
9, rue de la Michodière
75002 Paris
www.hoteldenoailles.com

OPPOSITE:
**Private terrace
adjoining an interior
courtyard suite.**

*I*T MAY LACK THE RENOWN of the neighboring 1st and 8th, but the 2nd arrondissement is a prime location for visitors. While not residential, the area is very Parisian and packed with discreet insider shopping destinations, theaters, nineteenth-century shopping arcades, and restaurants.

The Noailles is a case in point. It's situated on a narrow cross street between Opéra Garnier, place Vendôme, the Bourse stock exchange, and Bibliothèque Nationale, in a thriving business district that becomes delightfully calm in the evening. The Drouot auction houses are five minutes north, while the Palais Royal and Louvre museum are a short jaunt south. Owner and general manager Martine Falck is pleased to note that "the living is easy in this neighborhood—it's safe and calm, well serviced, and you can visit almost everything on foot." L'Usine, the most talked about sports club in the city with twenty coaches, a spa, and laundry service is directly opposite, and picturesque place Gaillon at the end of the block boasts two high-profile restaurants: the trendy Fontaine Gaillon, owned by film star Gerard Depardieu, and historic Drouant, with three-star chef Antoine Westerman.

Falck had an eye on the art deco hotel for some time before it came up for sale in 1990, which allowed time for her plans to germinate. She was working nearby at one of two hotels owned by her family and knew she was ready for her own. The hospitality gene is clearly active as Falck's daughter Florence Caresmel now helps her manage Noailles and granddaughter Justine is contemplating a degree from the prestigious Lausanne Hotel School.

A collector of French contemporary art, Falck made paintings, etchings, sculpture, and photography an integral design element. In addition to work on display throughout the ground-floor reception rooms, there is an original piece in every guest room, along corridors, on elevator landings, and in the small sitting areas on every floor. To promote a favorite artist, once a year the hotel hosts a temporary exhibition where work can be purchased.

Falck chose interior architect Jean-Luc Bras to bring to life her vision of a light-filled Zen environment that is "modern yet relaxed and gentle." Little remained but the name and facade of the old Parisian hotel when Noailles reopened in 1991. The purity of the concept has withstood the test of fashion and

OPPOSITE,
CLOCKWISE FROM TOP LEFT:
Bathroom overlooking
inner courtyard
with Philippe Stark-
designed tub.

Whimsical Ingo
Maurer hanging
lamp, dining room.

Detail, breakfast room.

Bedroom leads into
bathroom via frosted-
glass double doors.

Suite of paintings
by Maurice Douard,
reception sitting room.

with ongoing refurbishment the décor remains fresh. The core palette is composed of neutral gray, black, khaki, beige, and brown accented with red and terracotta. Design-edition furniture by Starck and Lissoni is sourced at Édifice, a design-furniture boutique on boulevard Raspail in the 7th, and the remaining furniture is custom made in Italy. Sleek, ash wood cupboards and wardrobes in guest rooms are standout designs. Sculptural light fixtures add decorative flair, especially the witty note holder chandelier by Ingo Maurer in the breakfast room.

At the back of the ground floor, off the breakfast room, is a large courtyard with exotic plantings. The garden is visible from the bar lounge through a glass wall configured like a Japanese screen. The ground floor is spacious and has several side reception rooms, making it easy to find a quiet nook. An inviting minimalist mezzanine off the bar has a fireplace faced with upholstered banquettes. Creative floral arrangements featuring exotic blooms and shapely leaves are another sculptural element within the décor. A large floral installation opposite the elevator in the lobby changes each week.

The breakfast buffet is an expansive spread that can be enjoyed in the spacious dining room or adjoining garden terrace. A private alfresco breakfast is an option if you book one of the first-floor guest rooms with a terrace enclosed by teak fences topped with greenery. Rooms and suites overlooking the central courtyard are especially quiet, and those on the higher floors get a good deal of daylight.

Imaginative use is made of frosted-glass partitions in lieu of opaque walls between bed and bathrooms to open up space. Clean lines, smooth textures, and blocks of neutral color establish a framework of restrained harmony against which artwork and one or two design elements with bolder personality come to life.

The sleek, well-stocked bar overlooking the garden terrace is open throughout the day until 10 p.m., and the hotel offers an abbreviated tasting menu until 11 p.m. More extensive room service may be called in from the kitchen of a small local restaurant between 8 p.m. and 3 a.m. A sauna and fitness center round out a range of amenities that is complete for a hotel of its size. Martine Falck is a stickler for service. "I'm happiest when we are praised for the thoroughness and sensitivity of our service. It's my 'war horse' and demands constant reinforcement and training for it to become second nature." Her effort is rewarded with a highly loyal clientele. In a competitive market, especially for business guests, Noailles has many repeat clients who book once a month throughout the year.

Whether you are visiting Paris for work or pleasure, Noailles provides a central location with easy access to just about everything you wish to see or do.

FITNESS
L'USINE

8, rue de la Michodière, 75002

Tel.: 01 42 66 30 30 | www.usineopera.com

A former factory transformed into an exclusive sports club described as "the perfect balance of sport, comfort, and elitism," with over seventy classes per week, from "boxe chic" to "spécial fessiers" (buttocks special), plus the latest equipment, coaching, steam room, sauna, and massage center. Being directly opposite, the hotel benefits from special access.

RESTAURANT
LA FONTAINE GAILLON

Place Gaillon, 75002

Tel.: 01 47 42 63 22 | www.la-fontaine-gaillon.com

Monday–Friday.

Gerard Depardieu's restaurant in a lovely historic landmark replete with fountain and outdoor terrace. The accent is on freshness and flavor with a seasonal menu and daily specials. The extensive wine list includes Depardieu's own château-bottled vintage.

RESTAURANT
DROUANT

16–18, place Gaillon, 75002

Tel.: 01 42 65 15 16 | www.drouant.com | reservations@drouant.com

Lunch and dinner.

Three-star Alsatian chef Alain Westermann has taken over this legendary location where the juries for France's premier literary prizes met to deliberate and award their honors. A remodeled interior and imaginative menu are breathing new life into a beloved institution.

HEALTH AND BEAUTY
MENARD INSTITUTE PARIS

21, rue de la Paix, 75002

Tel.: 01 42 65 58 08 | www.menard.fr

Monday–Saturday, 10 A.M.–7 P.M.

Beauty institute founded in Japan in 1959. The center offers body and facial treatments, manicures, and makeovers using its line of treatments and cosmetics.

RESTAURANT
CUISINE ET CONFIDENCES

33, place du Marché Saint-Honoré, 75001

Tel.: 01 42 96 31 34

The lunch spot where fashionable women rendezvous just off Faubourg Saint-Honoré. A *branché* address where the cuisine is spot-on and portions generous.

OPPOSITE CLOCKWISE FROM TOP LEFT:
Detail, austere chaperone,
bar, Duc de Saint Simon.

Detail, reception sitting room,
Pavillon de la Reine.

Romantic salon fireplace mantle,
Relais Christine.

Historic flavor

LE DUC DE SAINT-SIMON
(7th), Rue du Bac
Bourgeois charm

PAVILLON DE LA REINE
(3rd), Place des Vosges
Regal Marais residence

RELAIS CHRISTINE
(6th), Rue de Buci
Hôtel particulier with a legacy of hospitality

Time travel may be confined to dreams, but passing through the vaulted stone entryways of the Relais Christine and Pavillon de la Reine, guests segue into realms steeped in memory. The Historic Flavor section features three distinguished former private mansions that witnessed centuries of Parisian life starting with the ascendancy of the Bourbon dynasty in the seventeenth century—an epoch labeled *le Grand Siècle* because it is marked by fundamental developments in literature, diplomacy, religion, law, and education that continue to define French culture.

From the construction of Pont Neuf to the wedding celebration of Louis XIII and Anne of Austria in the place des Vosges and intrigue at the court of the Sun King documented by memoirist le Duc de Saint-Simon in Saint-Germain, the walls of these establishments and the surrounding streets are charged with a rich legacy of human drama.

LE DUC DE SAINT-SIMON

Bourgeois charm

Nouvel family
14, rue de Saint-Simon
75007 Paris
www.hotelducdesaintsimon.com

IF A HOTEL CAN CREATE THE ILLUSION of being a private club, the Saint-Simon does it rather convincingly, a feat that accounts for its appeal among those who abhor ambient music, noisy conversation, and anything promoted as new and different. This last the Duc de Saint-Simon is definitely not, and therein rests its charm. The front desk is still a table with four legs, and bookings were only recently computerized; tranquility and refinement trump technology in this historic end of the 7th arrondissement between boulevard Saint-Germain and the prime minister's headquarters at Hôtel Matignon.

Though the street and hotel bear the name of Louis IV's biographer, he lived a few blocks away on rue Saint-Dominique. The former Restoration mansion has the idiosyncratic layout of an old house, and guest rooms are correspondingly varied in proportion and mood. Rooms around the interior courtyard have pleasant views overlooking private gardens, and several open onto vine-covered terraces. If you aren't partial to floral and Jouy print wallpaper and fabric, the guestroom décor may not be your cup of tea, but those craving a dose of traditional *bon goût à la Française* should be sated. Many prints were customized for the hotel and, though a bit dated, they reinforce the impression that you are visiting well-to-do French relatives.

The building hasn't been substantially remodeled since it became a hotel in the 1920s catering to a British, Belgian, and French clientele. The guest profile hasn't altered significantly either. The occasional celebrity or fashion icon are outnumbered by titled Brits, French senators, and civil servants up from the provinces, as well as impeccably groomed couples of indeterminate age and nationality who come for the calm yet central location and bourgeois comforts. Lauren Bacall is said to appreciate the spacious ground-floor suite with an entry next to the front door allowing her to come and go incognito. Describing their clientele, Madame Zigelko, the seasoned director, tells the story of a particularly reserved guest who surprised her one morning with an embrace. When he checked in the prior evening, the night staff was new, and he'd been fearful that a complete change of the guard had occurred—threatening the predictability of his routine and treasured anticipation of his habits.

OPPOSITE:
French eighteenth-century portrait and headboard upholstered in Ralph Lauren fabric.

170

ABOVE, FROM LEFT:
Antique pendulum clock, salon.

Breakfast is served in a seventeenth-century vaulted stone cellar.

Portrait hanging in upper floor stairwell.

OPPOSITE TOP:
Built in corner couch, breakfast room.

OPPOSITE BOTTOM LEFT:
Salon walls are covered in elaborately pleated and swagged custom made fabric.

OPPOSITE BOTTOM RIGHT:
Sitting room, Suite 18.

The building's outstanding feature is a seventeenth-century cellar that pre-dates the rest of the building and is charmingly adapted. An elevator takes guests down to a cozy bar and breakfast room filled with antique furniture, paintings, and objects amassed by prior owners, one of whom was a professional antiques dealer and the other a passionate collector. Breakfast served on custom patterned Bernardaud Limoges is a civilized affair. The bar has two sections for optimum privacy—one facing the authentic zinc bar, and an alcove with upholstered bench covered with zodiac-symbol needlepoint pillows, and a collection of miniature mirrors with gilded frames hung overhead. Weather permitting, guests can have breakfast or relax over a beverage at sunset in the front courtyard.

Throughout the hotel, the arrangement of furniture and objects suggests gradual accumulation of a collection rather than clever decorator placement. Walking its corridors elicits a pleasant sense of anticipation knowing you are likely to come across an astonishing eighteenth-century portrait or a marquetry console. The quality of the artwork is unusually good, and there is a particularly fine seascape in the lobby.

You don't have to be a Francophile or culturally effete to appreciate the Duc de Saint-Simon's quintessentially Parisian allure. Once acclimated, the hotel's old world charm is apt to embrace you with a comforting aura of Proustian nostalgia.

GISELA ZIGELKO'S COUPS DE COEUR

GALLERY
LE VOLEUR D'IMAGES
Véronique de Folin
9, rue de Saint-Simon, 75007
Tel.: 01 45 51 07 77 | www.le-voleur-dimages.fr
Thursday–Saturday, 2 P.M.–7 P.M. and by appointment
Intimate gallery specializing in photography.

BOUTIQUE—PERFUME AND GLOVES
MAITRE PARFUMEUR ET GANTIER
84 bis, rue de Grenelle, 75007
Tel.: 01 45 44 61 57 | www.maire-parfumeur-et-gantier.com
Jean-Paul Millet Lage perpetuates a seventeenth-century royal
edict that designated the title master perfumer and glove maker.
His nostalgic range includes fragrances for women and men,
ambient perfumes, scented candles, and a line of gloves for
both sexes.

RESTAURANT
LA FERME SAINT-SIMON
6, rue de Saint-Simon, 75007
Tel.: 01 45 48 35 74
Closed Sunday.
Establishment spot frequented by editors, diplomats, and National
Assembly lawmakers. The décor is reminiscent of rural Normandy, and
the restaurant features a weekly market menu.

BOUTIQUE—WOMEN'S CLOTHING AND ACCESSORIES
SIMONE
1, rue de Saint-Simon, 75007
Tel.: 01 42 22 81 40 | simone@simoneruesaintsimone.com
A well-edited selection of young designer labels with a chic Left Bank
sensibility.

RESTAURANT
MAISON DE L'AMÉRIQUE LATINE
217, boulevard Saint-Germain – 75007
01 45 51 07 77 | www.mail217.org
Open for lunch year round and dinner May 1 through September 30.
Closed between Christmas and New Year, July 26 through August 25.
Housed in conjoined mansions overlooking beautiful private garden.
Candlelit dinner on the terrace in summer is idyllic. Bar menu is
Latin-American inspired. More formal restaurant serves Vincent
Limouzin's fine French cuisine. South American artists on exhibit in
adjoining salons.

PAVILLON DE LA REINE

Regal Marais residence

Chevalier family
28, place des Vosges
75003 Paris
www.pavillon-de-la-reine.com

*I*T IS HARD TO IMAGINE a more idyllic Parisian destination than the pavilion built to honor the royal marriage of Anne of Austria to Louis XIII on the place des Vosges, the capital's oldest square. In 1986, when Bertrand Chevalier, owner of Relais Christine, was scouting locations for his second hotel, the Marais had lost some of its *grande époche* luster, but with the Bastille opera house under construction to the east and historic mansions being converted into the Picasso and Carnavalet museums to the west, Chevalier anticipated an impending renaissance. His canny talent for trend spotting was confirmed by the hotel's immediate and ongoing success.

Pavillon de la Reine is secluded in a flowering courtyard behind a vaulted arcade at the north end of the square. The broad four-story building wrapped in Virginia creeper resembles the mansion of a county squire. Traversing the covered passageway into the open courtyard, guests transition into a privileged realm of light, air, and respite from urban buzz.

Place de Vosges was the first of Henri IV's urban-renewal projects and became a prototype for residential squares throughout continental Europe. The former place Royale was never a royal address but quickly became fashionable with the aristocracy. It remains the most beautiful, architecturally harmonious Parisian square, with a legacy of notable residents, the first of which was Cardinal Richelieu (number 21), who commissioned the original equestrian statue of Louis XIII. Number 6, home of Victor Hugo between 1832 and 1848, is now a city-run museum devoted to his memory.

The spirit and charm of the Relais Christine template was successfully transposed to its younger sister with the same warm, informal ambiance backed up by irreproachable courtesy and service. With locations on different banks of the Seine, the character and appeal of the two hotels have distinct points of difference. Pavillon manager Yves Monnin characterizes his guests as a "*Clientèle des créateurs*—conductors and musicians, artists, gallerists, fashion professionals, and people seeking an authentic cultural experience regardless of nationality. They come to decompress in the ambiance of a private residence where we know their habits and which room they prefer."

Iconic French fashion designer Jean-Paul Gaultier, who had an atelier nearby on rue du Faubourg Saint-Antoine, settled in for several years and offered

OPPOSITE:
Hotel façade in autumn, when clipped laurel, rosy Virginia creeper, and geranium-filled window boxes create the illusion of a country setting.

OPPOSITE LEFT:
In *Suite de la Reine*, designer Didier Benderli adds drama with seriograph enlargements of historic manuscripts.

OPPOSITE TOP RIGHT:
Sliding doors separate bedroom and sitting room, *Suite de la Reine*.

OPPOSITE BOTTOM RIGHT:
Catch a film on a screen inset in the bathroom wall while enjoying a restful soak.

suggestions for redecoration of his suite, the Victor Hugo, overlooking an interior Zen garden. One well-known photographer set up residence for six years until finally purchasing his own apartment on the square.

In 2008 a luxurious spa fitness center with massage and treatment facilities was inaugurated and ground-floor salons entirely refurbished. Breakfast is now served in light-filled reception rooms overlooking the front courtyard. A self-service "honor" bar by the fireplace is available throughout the day. Additional amenities include private parking and a seminar room.

Designer Didier Benderli is responsible for the interior. Each guest room is unique, and refurbishment takes place on a rotating basis, so he is able to maintain the contemporary classic style beloved by regular guests while introducing newer or more sophisticated elements.

A favored newlywed booking is the Suite de la Reine, with serigraph blowups of original handwritten manuscripts of the 1782 French classic *Les Liaisons Dangereuses* and a Rimbaud poem. The room's lofty proportions are accentuated by tall sliding doors separating the salon and bedroom and an oversize black chandelier suspended over the sitting area. A sofa upholstered in a creamy knitted fabric is echoed in the cream bedcover edged in chocolate velvet. The sumptuous second-floor suite has two bathrooms, one with inset television screen positioned so guests can watch a film while soaking in the clawfoot tub.

Pavillon de la Reine's staff understands that comfort is not simply material. Honesty, sensitivity, and sincerity are the accolades they value most—attributes that have built a solid reputation for this family hotel group.

YVES MONNIN'S COUPS DE COEUR

FLORIST
MAISON BAPTISTE
85, rue Vaneau, 75007
Tel.: 01 42 22 82 31
A florist with taste, talent, and sensitivity for enhancing an environment. He creates arrangements for the hotel as though it were a private home.

RESTAURANT
GASPARD DE LA NUIT
6, rue des Tournelles, 75004
Tel.: 01 42 77 90 53
Dining here is like eating at a friend's home. An address you'll want to keep secret, as it's rare to find a comparable mix of hospitality, simplicity, professionalism, and quality.

GOURMET—CHOCOLATE
JOSÉPHINE VANNIER
4, rue du Pas de la Mule, 75003
Tel.: 01 44 54 03 09 | www.chocolats-vannier.com
A veritable sculptress whose whimsical creations are beloved by gourmets and chocoholics and who is happy to fill custom orders.

MUSEUM
MUSÉE CARNAVALET
23, rue de Sévigné, 75003
Tel.: 01 4 59 58 58
Located in a former mansion of Madame de Sévigné, with some of the loveliest *jardins à la française* in Paris. Dedicated to relating the epic history of the city, its extraordinary growth, exceptional neighborhoods, and monuments.

ANTIQUES—MUSICAL INSTRUMENTS
ANDRÉ BISSONET
6, rue du Pas de la Mule, 75003
Tel.: 01 48 87 20 15 | andre.bissonnet@wanadoo.fr
A destination for music lovers, collectors, and aesthetes. You don't have to know how to play an instrument, since André Bissonet plays them all. His expertise and in-depth knowledge are equally impressive.

RELAIS CHRISTINE

Hôtel particulier with
a legacy of hospitality

Chevalier family
3, rue Christine
75006 Paris
www.relais-christine.com

WHEN IT OPENED IN 1980, Relais Christine set the standard for a new style of urban luxury hotel—intimate and idiosyncratic—that was soon labeled "boutique hotel" or *hôtel de charme.* A concept that is today universal provoked a seismic shift in the hospitality business at the time.

By establishing a neoclassical image from the start, the doyenne of the class has maintained its edge without having to reinvent itself or chase trends, while steadily refurbishing and expanding services. It helps to be endowed with exceptional physical assets including a spacious cobblestone forecourt, verdant rear garden, and gracious building with historic pedigree on a picturesque block with five solid restaurant options. Like a child who matures with a strong sense of self, Relais Christine exudes natural self-confidence. A high guest-to-staff ratio signals that management doesn't expect special-effects décor and technology to substitute for human contact, and an aura of seasoned professionalism puts guests immediately at ease. Don't be surprised if the person helping you decipher the Métro map tells you that they joined the staff twenty-five years ago and continues to enjoy their job. From Jean-Luc Chomat, the charming and exceedingly conscientious manager, on down through the ranks, the personnel are clearly proud of their hotel.

Relais Christine occupies a former residence dating from the early seventeenth century, though the entry facade facing the courtyard was rebuilt in 1898. The hotel's carriage logo implies that it served as a post house with a history of transient residents. Until its destruction in 1595, a building belonging to Grands-Augustins monks occupied the site, which was part of a complex extending to rue des Grands-Augustins. When Pont Neuf was constructed, Henri IV obliged the "hermit" monks to sell the building to accommodate new construction, and the street, rue Christine, is named for his daughter by Marie de Médicis.

Belowground, a preserved medieval kitchen or refectory is now the hotel dining room. The vaulted stone ceiling, massive central pillar, open fireplace, and well are reminders that the building has served as a communal residence for over seven hundred years.

The feel of the ground-floor salon at the rear of the main floor replicates the relaxed elegance of a private club. Furniture is arranged in casual groupings of

OPPOSITE:
Honeysuckle vines entwine the balustrade of Suite 31, overlooking the hotel garden.

ABOVE, FROM LEFT:
Tilted trio of lampshades, adjacent to elevator.

Substantial tasseled room key shouldn't be misplaced as easily as an electronic card.

Breakfast room, formerly a medieval kitchen.

OPPOSITE:
Unframed nineteenth-century portraits are hung throughout the wood-paneled salon.

sofas and armchairs around low tables—one of which displays a well-loved chess set. Glossy wood-paneled walls are hung with unframed late-nineteenth-century portraits of men who might have been sized up by the trim of their mustache or skill balancing a monocle and women who might have felt naked without a hat. The working fireplace and fully stocked "honor" bar are features becoming a rarity in Paris hotels.

Guest room décor remains faithful to the original concept in which each room is unique within an updated traditional French register. They are all being gradually refurbished, and the new decorator—while remaining faithful to the rooms' history—has injected a more contemporary spirit and palette. Ground-floor rooms that open onto the rear garden and have private terraces are a good choice for families with children, who can let off steam playing on the lawn.

As for mod cons, a new spa fitness center is one of the chicest in the city. After working out on the machines you can luxuriate in a spacious mosaic tile Jacuzzi, take a steam bath, or treat yourself to a pampering massage. Chomat regrets that so few clients take advantage of this aesthetically appealing retreat, especially since it is the perfect antidote to a busy day and not a resource that is often so readily accessible. Another hidden but nonetheless precious amenity is an underground garage in a neighborhood where street parking is limited.

The key to Relais Christine's success lies in the authenticity and charm of its ambiance and location combined with the solid quality of its service. Sensitivity to client satisfaction prevents complaisance and ensures that attention is paid to evolving expectations.

JEAN-LUC CHOMAT'S COUPS DE COEUR

RESTAURANT
ZE KITCHEN GALERIE
4, rue des Grands-Augustins, 75006
Tel.: 01 44 32 00 32 | www.zekitchengalerie.fr
Closed Saturday lunch and Sunday.
Rewarded in 2008 with a Michelin star, the Franco-Asian fusion cuisine
was already lauded by a discriminating Saint-Germain clientele and is
rumored to be among Alain Ducasse's preferred tables.

BOUTIQUE—CHILDREN'S CLOTHING
BOIS DE ROSE
30, rue Dauphine, 75006
Tel.: 01 40 46 04 24 | www.boisderose.krispen.fr
Monday–Saturday, 10:30 A.M.–7 P.M.
One of the last specialist suppliers of the smocked dresses and knee
britches worn by generations of French ring bearers and flower girls at
society weddings. Guaranteed to transform urchins into angels.

LANDMARK—CLASSICAL CONCERTS
SAINTE-CHAPELLE
4, boulevard du Palais, 75001
Tel.: 01 42 77 65 65
9:30 A.M.–6 P.M.
Brief classical concerts are staged in this exquisite chapel built by Louis
IX (later canonized) Thursday through Saturday evenings, featuring
quartets and soloists performing the great repertory. The ambiance
and acoustics are superb.

SIGHTSEEING
VEDETTES PONT-NEUF
Square du Vert-Galant, 75001
Tel.: 01 46 33 98 38 | www.vedettesdupontneuf.com
Sightseeing boat tour with commentary on the major monuments
between Nôtre Dame and Trocadéro. Especially magical at night when
all the monuments are illuminated.

SIGHTSEEING AND ENTERTAINMENT
YACHTS DE PARIS
Across from 10 bis, quai Henri IV, 75003
Tel.: 01 44 54 14 95 | www.yachtsdeparis.fr | contacts@yachtsdeparis.fr
Plan an unforgettable private party, reception, or dinner for two on one
of the yachts in this luxury fleet. The trip along the Seine can include a
stop-off at the Eiffel Tower.

Timeless elegance

FRANÇOIS 1ER
(8th), Rue François 1er
Homage to French culture and tradition

HÔTEL RAPHAEL
(16th), Étoile
A tradition of excellence

SAN REGIS
(8th), Grand Palais
Discretion and serenity

Concurrent with the development of railway travel, the nineteenth century witnessed the establishment of a hospitality industry. For the first time, hotels were designed to accommodate scores of guests, taking into account a desire for comfort, privacy, and entertainment. Architects outdid one another with plans for lavish reception rooms and the latest amenities, while the notion of providing excellent service for anyone who could afford the bill, rather than just the titled and privileged few, began to take hold.

The demand for palace hotels with cavernous ballrooms and hundreds of guest rooms has faded, but high standards and good manners never go out of style and the gilded legacy of this era is perpetuated in the three regal selections for Timeless Elegance.

Standing in the lobby of the Raphael or San Regis, it's a challenge to pinpoint evidence of the twenty-first century were it not for a passing guest accessorized with the latest Louis Vuitton or Dior handbag. The terms *traditional*, *conservative*, and *reassuring* come to mind, infused with the positive connotations these qualities embody with regard to professionalism. Each of these hotels serves as an indulgent antidote to cutting edge and the incessant pace of change.

FRANÇOIS 1ER

*Homage to French
culture and tradition*

Nouvel family
7, rue Magellan
75008 Paris
www.the-paris-hotel.com

F A HOTEL'S ULTIMATE MANDATE is to ensure that guests feel relaxed and well looked after, the François 1er accomplishes this mission the old-fashioned way, via attentive, professional service. A decade as general manager taught Alain Lagarrigue that client loyalty is developed through personal contact rather than eye-popping interior or technical bells and whistles. From the moment a guest at the François 1er crosses the marble lobby and settles into an armchair opposite a mahogany partners desk at the cozy reception area, a privileged status is conferred.

The international clientele appreciates the traditional yet stylish French interior design, intimate reception rooms, and discreet but omnipresent staff. Though not stodgy, there is a reassuring aura of gravitas, a patina of experience that comes off as pretentiousness at newer establishments with more to prove.

The hotel is named after France's Renaissance king and father of the French language (which became the lingua franca by decree in 1539). Francis I is also remembered for inviting Leonardo de Vinci in his twilight years to take up residence at his childhood home in Amboise. Masterpieces including the *Mona Lisa* bequeathed by the artist became the foundation of the French royal collection. A portrait of this cultured monarch (a copy of a Titian hanging in the Louvre) is displayed above a bouquet of roses in the entry hall—one of numerous Renaissance-themed decorative objects designer Pierre-Yves Rochon incorporated into the ground-floor salons.

A black Cararra marble floor inset with geometric green and red medallions lends a majestic aura to the lobby, which gives onto a sitting room adorned with a mélange of classical artwork, bronzes, and Asian bibelots. A striking reproduction of a Clouet portrait of Marguerite, queen of Navarre and sister of Francis I, hangs between the entry doors. Cream walls and subtle Oriental carpet against a pale parquet impart a fresh, graceful air. The side table bridging a pair of windows overlooking rue Magellan is well stocked with international newspapers and periodicals.

A secondary motif is trompe-l'oeil bookcases. The ground-floor elevator vestibule is lined with floor-to-ceiling leather spines that look like the real thing, and the bar alcove is papered with a more playful variation on the theme.

OPPOSITE:
Wall paneling painted to match the warm gold and red palette of a classic Jouy print.

ABOVE LEFT:
Guests are welcomed in
a private alcove with a
mahogany partner's desk.

ABOVE RIGHT:
Rouge Cardinale suite.

OPPOSITE TOP:
Front sitting room is
appointed with an eclectic
mix of Renaissance prints
and Chinese bibelots.

OPPOSITE BOTTOM
LEFT AND RIGHT:
Portraits of François 1er
and his sister Marguerite,
queen of Navarre.

OPPOSITE BOTTOM MIDDLE:
Details, breakfast room.

The secluded winter garden and adjoining bar are tailored for business appointments. You can envision cigar-smoking card players nursing brandy snifters in the clubby inner room (if smoking in hotel bars weren't strictly *interdit*). Mindful of the proximity of numerous international corporations and organizations, the hotel is equipped with two conference rooms. One appears suited for bankers or lawyers and the other for executives of a luxury-goods brand.

Guest-room ambiance is varied, but the color palette remains within a consistent range of warm red and buttery yellow, accented with gray and beige. Larger rooms tend to have fabric-covered walls, while standards have painted woodwork paneling. Fabrics include toile de Jouy, reeditions of eighteenth- and nineteenth-century floral prints, or tone-on-tone brocade and satin stripes. The effect is rich but tempered by the clean lines of black lacquer furniture and handsome framed engravings.

The surprise feature of the François 1er is its lovely breakfast room papered with a charming Pierre Frey design featuring orchids in blue and white cachepots. Framed prints of Chinese willow-pattern ginger jars, yellow tablecloths, and blue-and-white porcelain are perhaps inspired by the blue and yellow dining room of Monet's Giverny residence. Strategically placed columns create private nooks, some of which have sofa banquettes where you will be tempted to linger over the copious breakfast buffet.

If you are seeking a gilded refuge in a posh neighborhood where you can retreat at the close of a busy day, add the François 1er to your Paris hotel short list.

RESTAURANT

LE BISTRO DE L'OLIVIER

13, rue Quentin-Bauchart, 75008

Tel.: 01 47 20 17 00

Closed Saturday lunch and Sunday.

Best to reserve, especially for lunch, as this patch of Provence is a popular destination in a neighborhood short on bistros serving high-quality regional cooking.

BOUTIQUE—DESIGNER CLOTHING AND ACCESSORIES

VERSACE

41, rue François Ier, 75008

Tel.: 01 47 23 88 30

Of the many designer boutiques in the neighborhood, judging by shopping bags that pass through the lobby, Versace's Parisian outlet is the most frequented by hotel clientele.

GOURMET FOOD—BAKERY

BOULANGERIE JOSÉPHINE

69, avenue Marceau, 75116

Tel.: 01 47 20 49 62

An independent bakery with exceptional fruit tarts.

BOUTIQUE—REPRODUCTION PERIOD FURNITURE

MEUBLES TAILLARDAT

44, avenue Marceau, 75008

Tel.: 01 47 20 17 12 | showroom.taillardat@wanadoo.fr

www.taillardat.fr

If you don't have the budget for a signed Louis XV commode, this is where the Georges V, Plaza Athénée, and Château d'Yquem pick up reproductions. Since founding the company in 1987, Micheline Taillardat has expanded her eighteenth-century-inspired collection to two hundred pieces.

NIGHTCLUB

LE QUEEN

102, avenue des Champs-Élysées, 75008

Tel.: 01 53 89 08 90 | www.queen.fr

An institution that can take credit for reviving the avenue's appeal when nothing much was happening there in the 1980s. High rent now threatens to drive the club away. Monday Night Disco is a hoot.

HÔTEL RAPHAEL

A tradition of excellence

Bavarez family
17, avenue Kléber
750116 Paris
www.raphael-hotel.com

THE CATEGORY "PALACE" could have been coined for the Raphael. In 1925, after a quarter century as an acclaimed hotel entrepreneur, Leonard Tauber was determined to outdo himself. Despite their success, his other establishments—the art nouveau Régina off rue de Rivoli, opened for the 1900 Universal Exhibition, and the aptly named Majestic on avenue Kléber (since relocated)—were too large to be exclusive enough for *le ne plus ultra* clientele he wished to attract.

His dream was to create a super-luxury hotel with fewer but more spacious apartments and the ultimate in personalized service. Each of the ninety guest rooms was appointed with a spacious sitting room, intimate bed alcove, lavish built-in wardrobes, and a bathroom with the latest amenities. In a testament to the quality of workmanship and artistry of the decoration, many of the suites remain essentially as they were when the hotel opened and as such rank among the most atmospheric period interiors in the city. Tauber kept the top floor to himself, and today the salons and library of his former apartment—with wraparound terraces overlooking the Arc de Triomphe—are available for banquets and receptions.

A voracious collector of art and antiques, Tauber filled the lobby gallery and salons with sumptuous furniture, oil paintings, carpets, bronzes, and bibelots. The jewel of the collection is a Turner landscape, which hangs somewhat discreetly opposite the magnificent elevator, treating guests to a glimpse of an era when even elevator travel was designed for repose and aesthetic pleasure.

After dedicating his life to the embellishment and management of hotels, Tauber bequeathed his empire to business associate Constant Bavarez. Today the Raphael is the last family-owned and managed Parisian Palace hotel. Françoise Bavarez, who inherited her grandfather's dedication to service and luxury, is sensitive to the responsibility of preserving the hotel's treasures while updating room décor and expanding services to meet to the needs of a twenty-first-century clientele.

Who would dare tamper with the clubby plush red velvet English Bar, which buzzes nonstop from breakfast meetings through to the after-dinner drinks crowd? The bar's popularity led management to open the adjoining Lounge 17 as

OPPOSITE:
Bed alcove paneled in eighteenth-century *boiseries, Raphael* triplex suite.

OPPOSITE LEFT:
The *Raphael* suite was the residence of Raphael's founder, Leonard Tauber.

OPPOSITE TOP RIGHT:
Corner table, hotel restaurant.

OPPOSITE BOTTOM RIGHT:
Suite bar stocked with *grand cru* Bordeaux wine.

a less formal dining alternative to the elegant restaurant. In fair weather, one of the loveliest places in Paris for drinks or a romantic meal is the rooftop terrace garden with its panoramic view of the city. For landscaping alone it scores top marks. The privileged few who book the Raphael duplex incorporating Tauber's bedroom suite with exquisite eighteenth-century chinoiserie paneling can scale the oak stairwell to an office with stained-glass window, then head further up to the rooftop pavilion opening onto a private terrace featuring an enormous sculptural chess set. The landscaped two-thousand-square-foot terrace is an incomparable setting for a private party or special celebration.

Since its inception, the Raphael has been a retreat for so many stars and famous personalities that it's impossible to create an abbreviated list without trivializing the depth of the roster. Over 650 international celebrities have checked in; some, like Serge Gainsbourg, who moved in while his Saint-Germain house was being worked on, stay for months at a stretch. Over sixty films have had scenes shot at the hotel, and it remains a favored rendezvous for celebrity press interviews because of an impeccable reputation for discretion.

The hotel is especially popular with diplomatic delegations because the French state department designates it as meeting the highest standards of security. I wasn't surprised to pass a distinguished financier and former American ambassador on the way in. Lionel, the charming concierge who joined the hotel staff thirty years ago and is currently vice-president of the French concierge association, was reluctant to confirm my sighting but did admit that the gentleman had switched allegiance from a glitzier establishment because "he feels more at home here."

Though mercurial trends are as cruel to hotel status as to fashion labels, the Raphael, like all classics, has maintained its low-key cachet by remaining true to the vision of excellence inculcated by its founder.

LEFT TOP:
L'Arc de Triomphe
view, roof terrace.

LEFT BOTTOM:
The roof garden
restaurant is landscaped
for optimal privacy.

OPPOSITE:
Lounge "17" proposes
a light lunch menu.

OVERLEAF,
LEFT AND TOP RIGHT:
Chantilly elegance of
Arc de Triomphe suite,
favored by newlyweds.

LANDMARK
PLACE DES ÉTATS-UNIS, 75016

A graceful square with monuments commemorating Franco-American *amitié* from the time of Washington and Lafayette, including a tree honoring victims of 9/11/2001. Surrounding mansions include the former American embassy at number 16 and Hôtel de Noailles at number 11, recently purchased by Baccarat Crystal and renovated by Philippe Starck to house an extravagant showroom, museum, and Cristal Room restaurant.

MUSEUM
MUSÉE GUIMET

6, place d'Iéna, 75116
www.guimet.fr
10:00 A.M.–6:00 P.M.; closed Tuesday.
The National Museum of Asiatic Art, initially devoted to the religions of ancient Egypt, classical antiquity, and Asia, has one of the finest specialist collections in France. The permanent collection may be visited free of charge.

TEA SALON
CARETTE

4, place du Trocadéro (by avenue Kléber), 75116
Tel.: 01 47 27 88 56
An institution that was recently renovated and lays claim to the best chocolate éclair in the city among other sweet and savory delights. Light, airy space with a broad terrace offering a pleasant view of the museums on the other side of the *place*.

WALK
BANKS OF THE RIVER SEINE

Dedicate half a day to a stroll east from the Pont de l'Alma to Notre Dame and back, crossing over bridges as you go to take in first-rate panoramas.

SHOPPING STREET
AVENUE VICTOR HUGO, 75016

Window shop or browse along this exceptional stretch of boutiques between place Victor Hugo and place de l'Étoile.

SAN REGIS

Discretion and serenity

Georges family
12, rue Jean-Goujon
75008 Paris
www.hotel-sanregis.com

A HAVEN OF DISCREET LUXURY at the nexus of haute couture and high art, the San Regis embodies a French proverb, "To live well, live hidden." The residential tranquility of its location lets one forget that avenue Montaigne designer boutiques, the Grand-Palais exhibition hall, and bustle of the Champs Élysées are just a stroll away. It's a given that the neighborhood is exclusive when the townhouse opposite is the private investment headquarters of François Pinault, billionaire luxury-brand mogul and art collector.

An ornate wrought-iron marquee and flower-filled window boxes enliven the sober limestone facade. The entry is flanked to the right by a reception desk tucked out of view and to the left by a miniature waiting room reminiscent of the vestibules women are parked in at men's clubs. A flight of marble steps leads to the inner sanctum, which radiates the cozy splendor and perennial chic of an haut-bourgeois Parisian townhouse. The San Regis manages to be luxurious and traditional while evading the impersonal opulence of a palace hotel. Its suite of intimate salons and jewel-box dining room are richly furnished like the home of a collector with a passion for beautiful objects and antique craftsmanship. The relaxed atmosphere evokes a reassuring sense of familiarity—a time capsule that has seduced discerning travelers since fashion editor Carmel Snow used it as a *Bazaar* magazine outpost in the 1950s and Hollywood icons, statesmen, CEOs, and celebrated artists first made it their pied à terre.

Built in 1857 as a private residence, it was converted to a hotel in 1923 by Simon-André Terrail (whose son owns the fabled Tour d'Argent restaurant). Terrail purchased the building after selling the neighboring Georges V, bringing with him the pick of its period furniture and collectibles. In the early 1980s, when it badly needed modernization, Elie Georges—a businessman with a passion for art and antiques—bought the hotel and set to restoring and supplementing its treasures from his own collection while upgrading the infrastructure to the standards of a palace hotel.

The historic link with neighboring Georges V was perpetuated by interior designer Pierre-Yves Rochon, who created the San Regis's new look during major renovations in 1985 and 1986 and further remodeling in 1995. Based on the acclaim of his work, he went on to oversee refurbishment of the Georges V.

OPPOSITE:
Suite 10 is a symphony of crisp china-blue.

OPPOSITE LEFT:
Sliding doors separate
bedroom and sitting
room of Suite 10.

OPPOSITE RIGHT,
TOP TO BOTTOM:
An elegant pair of
lanterns flanking the
elaborate marquis create
a distinguished entry.

Golden-hued Suite 24 is
among the most spacious.

The sitting room of Suite
61, which has a beautiful
balcony view.

OVERLEAF, BOTTOM RIGHT:
Jewel-box dining room
with trompe l'oeil
bookshelves.

The décor of every room is unique within a classic register in keeping with the hotel's heritage. Customized fabrics by Canovas, Frey, and Branquenié predominate in shades of warm red, golden yellow, and blue. Outstanding features are spacious walk-in closets or dressing rooms, period furniture, and attention paid to the selection of one-of-a-kind lamps and porcelain vases. Several suites on the upper floors have terraces with superb views of the Eiffel Tower and the soaring fin-de-siècle greenhouse roofline of the Grand Palais. Hallways are as tastefully appointed as the rooms, and nineteenth-century stained-glass windows illuminate the gracious stairwell.

If the San Regis exudes a spirit of serenity, it's transmitted by the gentle, attentive manner of the owners and their experienced staff. The personnel, many of whom worked under prior ownership, have an attachment to the establishment that is akin to family pride. This quality of service has created a roster of repeat guests. One couple, after booking the same suite for years, were consulted about their preferences prior to redecoration, to ensure they'd continue to feel at home. Clients return as old friends and relish the familial attention reflected in every aspect of the hotel's amenities.

Elie Georges leaves marketing and management to his brothers Maurice and Joseph while continuing to oversee décor. His son Charles, a recent business school graduate, is sales executive. Describing how his father nurtured in him an appreciation for art and antiques, he explained that many of the hotel's decorative objects and furniture are transplants from home. "My father likes to live with things until he decides the right place for them at the hotel."

The restaurant—available to guests for breakfast, lunch, and dinner—is popular with locals for a quiet business breakfast or tête-à-tête lunch. With seating for twenty or so, the proportions are those of a private dining room. The Empire fireplace, trompe-l'oeil bookcases, and walls upholstered in Pierre Frey print create a hideaway ambiance. The classic cuisine is very good, and thanks to a lack of pretension it isn't too pricey. Other special services are round-the-clock room service and a bar in the atrium salon, serving until 11 p.m.

Being a world-class hotel, the requisite technological amenities are available, but nothing is rushed or hard-edged here—which gives the San Regis the distinction of being a true refuge from the dissonance of urban life.

ELLIE GEORGES'S COUPS DE COEUR

BOUTIQUE—DESIGNER CLOTHING AND ACCESSORIES
DIOR
30, avenue Montaigne, 75008
Tel.: 01 40 73 73 73
Headquarters and birthplace of a French brand that has expanded since 1947 to attain the greatest recognition of any luxury fashion name.

AUCTION HOUSE
CHRISTIE'S PARIS
9, avenue Matignon, 75008
Tel.: 01 40 76 85 85 | www.cristies.com
Monday–Friday, 10 A.M.–6 P.M.
One of Ellie George's preferred destinations for indulging his love of art and expert craftsmanship.

MONUMENTS
THE GRAND AND PETIT PALAIS
Avenue Winston Churchill, 75008
www.grandpalais.fr | www.petitpalais.paris.fr
Built for the Universal Exposition of 1900, the Grand Palais continues to host major exhibitions and fairs including the FIAC contemporary art fair. The Petit Palais is now the Paris Beaux Arts Museum. The architecture and interiors of the buildings are works of art in their own right.

RESTAURANT
LASSERRE
17, avenue Franklin Roosevelt, 75008
Tel.: 01 43 59 53 43
www.restaurant-lasserre.com | lasserre@lassserre.fr
Founded and managed by Réne Lasserre from 1942 to 2006. Classic haute cuisine in an elegant setting conveniently close to the hotel.

ENTERTAINMENT
THÉÂTRE DES CHAMPS-ÉLYSÉES
15, avenue Montaigne, 75008
Tel.: 01 49 52 50 50 | www.theatrechampselysees.fr
Recommended for the exceptional quality and variety of the artistic program featuring classical music, jazz, world music, opera, and dance. The art deco building is a historic landmark.

INDEX: HOTELS

BROCANTE CHIC

CHÂTEAUBRIAND
Romain Rio
6, rue Châteaubriand
75008 Paris
FRANCE
Tel.: 33 (0)1 40 76 00 50
Fax: 33 (0)1 40 76 09 22
www.hotelchateaubriand.com
welcome@hotelchateaubriand.com
Métro: Charles de Gaulle "Étoile"
28 rooms
Rate: Mid-price to luxury
Breakfast: €18+

LE LAVOISIER
Michel Bouvier
21, rue Lavoisier
75008 Paris
FRANCE
Tel.: 33 (0)1 53 30 06 06
Fax: 33 (0)1 53 30 23 00
Toll-free number: +1 866 376 7831
        (USA/Canada)
www.hotellavoisierparis.com
info@hotellavoisier.com
Métro: Saint-Augustin
30 rooms including 1 suite
        and 3 junior suites
Rate: Moderate to mid-price
Breakfast: 14€

SAINT VINCENT
Bertrand Plasmans
5, rue du Pré-aux-Clercs
75007 Paris
FRANCE
Tel.: 33 (0)1 42 61 01 51
Fax: 33 (0)1 42 61 01 54
www.hotel-st-vincent.com
reservation@hotelstvincent.com
Métro: Saint-Germain-des-Prés
Rate: Moderate to mid-price
Breakfast: €13

WINDSOR HOME
Frédéric Barazer
3, rue Vital
750016 Paris
FRANCE
Tel.: 33 (0)1 45 04 49 49
Fax: 33 (0)1 45 04 59 50
www.windsorhomeparis.fr
infos@windsorhomeparis.fr
Métro: Passy
8 rooms
Rate: Moderate
Breakfast: 11€

BOUDOIR

LE DANIEL
Nammour family
8, rue Frederic Bastiat
75008 Paris
FRANCE
Tel.: 33 (0)1 42 56 17 00
Fax: 33 (0)1 42 56 17 01
www.hoteldanielparis.com
reservation@hoteldanielparis.com
Métro: Saint-Philippe du Roule
22 rooms and 4 suites
Rate: Luxury
Breakfast: €22 and €30
Restaurant and bar lounge

L'HÔTEL
Peter Frankopan
13, rue des Beaux Arts
75006 Paris
FRANCE
Tel.: 33 (0)1 44 41 99 00
Fax: 33 (0)1 43 25 64 81
www.l-hotel.com
e.stay@l-hotel.com
Métro: Saint-Germain-des-Prés
16 rooms and 4 suites
Rate: Luxury
Breakfast: €20
Restaurant and bar lounge

VILLA D'ESTRÉE
Chevance family
17, rue Gît le Coeur
75006 Paris
FRANCE
Tel.: 33 (0)1 55 42 71 11
Fax: 33 (0)1 55 42 71 00
www.villadestrees.com
resa@villadestrees.com
Métro: Saint-Michel
10 rooms in villa and 11 in residence
Rate: Mid-price
Breakfast: €12
Restaurant: Café Latin

DESIGN CLASSICS

DOKHAN'S
Dokhan family
117, rue Lauriston
75116 Paris
FRANCE
Tel.: 33 (0)1 53 65 66 99
Fax: 33 (0)1 53 65 66 88
www.dokhans.com
reservation@dokhans.com
Métro: Trocadéro
41 rooms and 4 suites
Rate: Luxury
Breakfast: €16 and €27
Champagne bar

KEPPLER
Nouvel family
10, rue Kepler
75016 Paris
FRANCE
Tel.: 33 (0)1 47 20 65 05
Fax: 33 (0)1 47 23 02 29
www.keppler.fr
hotel@keppler.fr
Métro: Georges V
33 rooms & 5 suites
Rate: Luxury
Breakfast: 14€ continental, 22€ buffet

SEZZ
Shahé Kalaidjian
6, avenue Frémiet
75016 Paris
FRANCE
Tel.: 33 (0)1 56 75 26 26
Fax: 33 (0)1 56 75 26 16
www.hotelsezz.com
mail@hotelsezz.com
Métro: Passy
13 rooms and 14 suites
Rate: Luxury
Breakfast: €25

LE PLACIDE
Jean Pierre Bansard
6, rue Saint-Placide
75006 Paris
FRANCE
Tel.: 33 (0)1 42 84 34 60
Fax: 33 (0)1 47 20 79 78
www.leplacidehotel.com
contact@leplacidehotel.com
Métro: Sèvres-Babylone
11 rooms (1 handicap access duplex)
Rate: Mid-price to luxury
Breakfast: €22

COUTURE

5, RUE DE MOUSSY
Azzedine Alaia
5, rue de Moussy
75004 Paris
FRANCE
Tel.: 33 (0)1 44 78 92 00
Fax: 33 (0)1 42 76 08 48
www.3rooms-5ruedemoussy.com
info@3rooms-5ruedemoussy.com
Métro: Hôtel de Ville
3 apartments: 2 two-bedroom and 1
    one-bedroom
Rate: Luxury for one person but is mid-
    price for 2 or 3 people with €50 sur-
    charge for each additional guest
Breakfast: €28

HÔTEL DU PETIT MOULIN
Nadia Murano
29/31, rue de Poitue
75003 Paris
FRANCE
Tel.: 33 (0)1 42 74 10 10
Fax: 33 (0)1 42 74 10 97
www.hoteldupetitmoulin.com
contact@hoteldupetitmoulin.com
Métro: Filles du Calvaire or Saint-
    Sebastién–Froissart
17 rooms
Rate: Mid-price
Breakfast: €15
Bar lounge

BAR LOUNGE

GÉNÉRAL
Gilles Douillard
5/7, rue Rampon
75011 Paris
FRANCE
Tel.: 33 (0)1 47 00 41 57
Fax: 33 (0)1 47 00 21 56
Legeneralhotel.com
resa@legeneralhotel.com
Métro: Oberkampf
46 rooms
Rate: Moderate to mid-price
Breakfast: €16
Bar lounge

HÔTEL DE BANVILLE
Marianne Moreau
166, boulevard Berthier
75017 Paris
FRANCE
Tel.: 33 (0)1 42 67 70 16
Fax: 33 (0)1 44 40 42 77
www.hotelbanville.fr
info@hotelbanville.fr
Métro: Porte de Champeret
38 rooms and 1 suite
Rate: Mid-price
Breakfast: €20
Bar lounge

KUBE
Groupe Murano
1–5, passage Ruelle
75018 Paris
FRANCE
Tel.: 33 (0)1 42 05 20 00
Fax: 33 (0)1 42 05 21 01
www.kubehotel.com
paris@kubehotel.com
Métro: La Chapelle
41 rooms and suites
Rate: Mid-price to luxury
Breakfast: €25
Restaurant and bar lounge

DE SERS
Thibault Vidalenc
41, avenue Pierre 1er de Serbie
75008 Paris
FRANCE
Tel.: 33 (0)1 53 23 75 75
Fax: 33 (0)1 53 23 75 76
www.hoteldesers.com
contact@hoteldesers.com
Métro: Georges V
45 rooms and 6 suites
Rate: Luxury
Breakfast: €29 to €35
Restaurant and bar lounge

LITERARY

GRANDS HOMMES
Corinne Moncelli
17 place du Pantheon
75005 Paris
FRANCE
Tel.: 33 (0) 1 46 34 19 60
Fax: 33 (0) 1 43 26 67 32
www.hoteldesgrandshommes.com
reservation@hoteldesgrandeshommes.com
Métro: Luxembourg
31 rooms
Rate: Moderate to mid-price
Buffet breakfast: €12

PONT ROYAL

Leroy family
7, rue de Montalembert
75007 Paris
FRANCE
Tel.: 33 (0)1 42 84 70 00
Fax: 33 (0)1 42 84 71 00
www.hotel-pont-royal.com
hpr@hotel-pont-royal.com
Métro: Rue du Bac
65 rooms, 9 junior suites, and
    1 panoramic suite
Rate: Luxury
Restaurant: L'Atelier de Joël Robuchon
and bar lounge

RELAIS SAINT-GERMAIN

Claudine and Yves Camdeborde
9, carrefour de l'Odéon
75006 Paris
FRANCE
Tel.: 33 (0)1 44 27 07 97
Fax: 33 (0)1 46 33 45 30
www.hotelrsg.com
hotelrsg@wanadoo.fr
Métro: Odéon
Rate: Mid-price
Breakfast: €14
Restaurant: Le Comptoir

CONTEMPORARY ART
·······························

LE A

Sorman family
4, rue d'Artois
75008 Paris
FRANCE
Tel.: 33 (0)1 42 56 99 99
Fax: 33 (0)1 42 56 99 90
www.hotel-le-a-paris.com
hotel-le-a@wanadoo.fr
Métro: Saint-Philippe du Roule
16 rooms and 10 suites
Rate: Luxury
Breakfast: €22
Bar lounge

DES ACADEMIES ET DES ARTS

Charlotte and Laurent Inchauspé
15, rue de la Grande Chaumière
75006 Paris
FRANCE
Tel.: 33 (0)1 43 26 66 44
Fax: 33 (0)1 40 46 86 85
hoteldesacademies.com
reservation@hoteldesacademies.com
Métro: Vavin
Rate: Mid-price
20 rooms
Breakfast: €15

HÔTEL PARTICULIER MONTMARTRE

Morgane Rousseau
23, avenue Junot
75018 Paris
FRANCE
Tel.: 33 (0)1 53 41 81 40
www.hotel-particulier-montmartre.com
hotelparticulier@orange.fr
Métro: Lamarck–Caulaincourt
5 suites
Rate: Luxury
Breakfast: Included
Dinner: Upon request

NOAILLES

Martine Falck
9, rue de la Michodière
75002 Paris
FRANCE
Tel.: 33 (0)1 47 42 92 90
Fax: 33 (0)1 49 24 92 71
www.hoteldenoailles.com
goldentulip.denoailles@wanadoo.fr
Métro: Opéra
59 rooms
Rate: Mid-price to luxury
Breakfast: €15

HISTORIC FLAVOR
·······························

LE DUC DE SAINT-SIMON

Nouvel family
14, rue Saint-Simon
75007 Paris
FRANCE
Tel.: 33 (0)1 44 39 20 20
Fax: 33 (0)1 45 48 68 25
www.hotelducdesaintsimon.com
duc.du.saint.simon@wanadoo.fr
Métro: Rue du Bac
33 rooms and 1 suite
Rates: Mid-price
Breakfast: €15

PAVILLON DE LA REINE

Chevalier family
28, place des Vosges
75003 Paris
FRANCE
Tel.: 33 (0)1 40 29 19 19
Fax: 33 (0)1 40 29 19 20
www.pavillon-de-la-reine.com
contact@pavillon-de-la-reine.com
Métro: Bastille
41 rooms and 15 suites
Rate: Luxury
Breakfast: €25

RELAIS CHRISTINE

Chevalier family
3, rue Chrisine
75006 Paris
FRANCE
Tel.: 33 (0)1 40 51 60 80
Fax: 33 (0)1 40 51 60 80
www.relais-christine.com
contact@relais-christine.com
Métro: Odéon
29 rooms, 2 terrace suites, 5 junior
    suites, and 11 duplex suites
Rate: Luxury
Breakfast: €25 and €30

TIMELESS ELEGANCE

FRANÇOIS 1ER
Nouvel family
7, rue Magellan
75008 Paris
FRANCE
Tel.: 33 (0)1 47 23 44 04
Fax: 33 (0)1 47 23 93 43
www.the-paris-hotel.com
hotel@hotel-francois1er.fr
Métro: Georges V
Rate: Luxury
Breakfast: €21

HÔTEL RAPHAEL
Bavarez family
17, avenue Kléber
750116 Paris
FRANCE
Tel.: 33 (0)1 53 64 32 00
Fax: 33 (0)1 53 64 32 01
www.raphael-hotel.com
management@raphael-hotel.com
Métro: Kléber
65 rooms and 25 suites
Rate: Luxury to deluxe
Breakfast: €37
Restaurants and bar lounge

SAN REGIS
Georges family
12, rue Jean-Goujon
75008 Paris
FRANCE
Tel.: 33 (0)1 44 95 16 16
Fax: 33 (0)1 45 61 05 48
www.hotel-sanregis.com
message@hotel-sanregis.com
Métro: Franklin D. Roosevelt
44 rooms (3 suites)
Rate: Luxury to deluxe
Restaurant and bar lounge

INDEX: COUPS DE COEUR

Compilation by category for ease of reference. Page number next to the name of destination refers back to the full description.

Gastronomic
LASSERRE, 209
17, avenue Franklin Roosevelt,
75008
Tel.: 01 43 59 53 43

Gastronomic
SENDERENS, 17
9, place de la Madeleine, 75008
Tel.: 01 42 65 22 90

Asian
GINGER, 120
11, rue de Trémoille, 75008
Tel.: 01 47 23 37 32

Bistro
ASTIER, 100
44, rue Jean-Pierre Timbaud, 75011
Tel.: 01 43 57 16 35

Seafood
LA MARÉE PASSY, 28
71, avenue Paul Doumer, 75016
Tel.: 01 45 04 12 81

Brasserie-Bistro
LE SCHEFFER, 28
22, rue Scheffer, 75016
Tel.: 01 47 27 81 11

Bistro
LA TABLE LAURISTON, 59
129, rue Lauriston, 75016
Tel.: 01 47 27 00 07

Contemporary French
CAFÉ DE L'HOMME, 59
Musée de l'Homme
17, place du Trocadéro, 75116
Tel.: 01 44 05 30 15

Japanese
AKASAKA, 71
9, rue Nicolo, 75016
Tel.: 01 42 88 77 86

Contemporary French
**THE CRISTAL ROOM–
BACCARAT**, 59
11, place des États-Unis, 75116
Tel.: 01 40 22 11 10

Bistro
PHÉBÉ, 107
190, rue de Courcelles, 75017
Tel.: 01 46 22 33 23

Contemporary French
BALTHAZAR, 107
73, avenue Niel, 75017
Tel.: 01 44 40 28 15

Traditional
**LE MOULIN DE
LA GALETTE**, 113
83, rue Lepic, 75018
Tel.: 01 46 06 84 77

Bistro
LUI…L'INSOLENT, 113
15, rue Caulaincourt, 75018
Tel.: 01 53 28 28 31

Gastronomic
**LE COTTAGE
MARCADET**, 113
151 bis, rue Marcadet, 75018
Tel.: 01 42 57 71 22

TEA SALONS

1728, 17
8, rue d'Anjou, 75008
Tel.: 01 40 17 07 77

LA CHARLOTTE DE L'ISLE, 17
24, rue St. Louis en l'Ile, 75004
Tel.: 01 45 54 25 83

**LADURÉE CHAMPS
ÉLYSÉES**, 148
75, avenue des Champs Élysées,
75008
Tel.: 01 40 75 08 75

CARETTE, 203
4, place du Trocadéro (by avenue
Kléber), 75116
Tel.: 01 47 27 88 56

BARS

Café Bar
LE PROGRESS, 93
1, rue de Bretagne, 75003
Tel.: 01 42 72 01 44

Wine Bar Restaurant
**CAFÉ DE LA
NOUVELLE MAIRIE**, 129
19–21, rue des Fossés Saint
Jacques, 75005
Tel.: 01 44 07 04 41

Bar Restaurant
LE BRISTOL, 148
112, rue du Faubourg Saint-
Honoré, 75008
Tel.: 01 53 43 43 00

After Hours
CAFÉ CHARBON, 100
109, rue Oberkampf, 75011
Tel.: 01 43 57 57 40

Bar Bistro
CLOWN BAR, 100
114, rue Amelot, 75011
Tel.: 01 43 55 87 35

LE ROSEBUD, 155
11 bis, rue Delambre, 75014
Tel.: 01 42 35 38 54

GOURMET FOOD

Covered Market and Eateries
**LE MARCHÉ DES
ENFANTS-ROUGES**, 93
39, rue de Bretagne, 75003

Ice Cream
MAISON BERTHILLON, 85
29–31, rue Saint Louis en l'Île,
75004
Tel.: 01 43 54 31 61

Butcher
BOUCHERIE GARDIL, 85
44, rue Saint Louis en l'Île, 75004
Tel.: 01 43 54 97 15

Chocolate
JOSÉPHINE VANNIER, 181
4, rue du Pas de la Mule, 75003
Tel.: 01 44 54 03 09

Charcuterie
**CHARCUTERIE
DU PANTHÉON**, 129
200, rue Saint Jacques, 75005
Tel.: 01 43 54 24 48

Tea
MARRIAGE FRÈRES, 51
13, rue des Grands Augustins,
75006
Tel.: 01 40 51 82 50

L'EPICERIE, 23
22, rue des Saints-Pères, 75006
Tel.: 01 42 96 90 02

Cheese
ANDROUET, 135
37, rue de Verneuil, 75007
Tel.: 01 42 61 97 55

Chocolate
**LA MAISON DU
CHOCOLAT**, 65
52, rue François 1er, 75008
Tel.: 01 47 23 38 25

HÉDIARD, 17
21, place de la Madeleine, 75008
Tel.: 01 43 12 88 88

Bakery
BOULANGERIE KAYSER, 39
85, boulevard Malsherbes, 75008
Tel.: 01 45 22 70 30

Café, Culinary Boutique,
and Cooking School
LENÔTRE, 59
48, avenue Victor Hugo, 75116
Tel.: 01 45 02 21 21

Chocolate
PATRICK ROGER, 28
45, avenue Victor Hugo, 75116
Tel.: 01 45 01 66 71

Bakery
**BOULANGERIE
JOSÉPHINE**, 195
69, avenue Marceau, 75116
Tel.: 01 47 20 49 62

Covered market
MARCHÉ DE PASSY, 107
Corner of rue Bois-le-Vent, 75106

Bakery
**R. MAEDER–BOULANGERIE
PATISSERIE ALSACIENNE**, 00
158, boulevard Berthier, 75017
Tel.: 01 46 22 50 73

FLORISTS

PASCAL MUTEL, 140
6, Carrefour de l'Odéon, 75006
Tel.: 01 43 26 02 56

OLIVIER PITOU, 23
14, rue des Saints-Pères, 75006
Tel.: 01 49 27 97 49

L'ARTISAN FLEURISTE, 77
6, rue de Commaille, 75007
Tel.: 01 42 84 40 41

MAISON BAPTISTE, 181
85, rue Vaneau, 75007
Tel.: 01 42 22 82 31

DESIGNER
BOUTIQUES

BALENCIAGA, 65
10, avenue Georges V, 75008
Tel.: 01 47 20 21 11

DIOR, 209
30, avenue Montaigne, 75008
Tel.: 01 40 73 73 73

Casey O'Brien Blondes is the author of *French Country Hideaways*. She moved to France from the U.S. in 1988 and lives between Touraine and Paris. *cobrienblondes@gmail.com*